LOVING EDUCATION

Restoring the Heart of Education

By Anton Anthony

Denver, Colorado, USA

Anton Anthony
Contact@AuthorAntonAnthony.com
209 Horseshoe Circle
Waynesboro GA 30830
United States

Ordering Information:

Quantity sales. Special discounts are available on quantity purchases by corporations, associations, and others. For details, contact the publisher at the address above.

Printed in the United States of America

Publisher's Cataloging-in-Publication data

Anthony, Anton.
Loving Education : Restoring the Heart of Education / Anton Anthony published by 40 Day Writer LLC.
p. 194

ISBN: 978-1-9486720-2-3 (hardback)
ISBN: 978-1-9486720-7-8 (paperback)
ISBN: 978-1-9486720-1-6 (eBook)

1. Education
2. Interpersonal Relationships
3. Educational Reform.

First Edition
14 13 12 11 10 / 10 9 8 7 6 5 4 3 2 1

DEDICATION

There are a lot of people who mean the world to me, including Charlice, Malik, Mikal, Anton Jr., my father Roosevelt Anthony, my brothers, Jay and Octavian. But this book is dedicated to my mother, Lynda Anthony.

I believe in giving people flowers while they are still living, and I want to give her flowers while she is still alive. She has supported me throughout my life, and I owe the world to her. To a woman who will give her last to anyone she loves. Thank you, Mom, for always being there for me.

TABLE OF CONTENTS

INTRODUCTION

"*I have a dream that one day every educator would care more about the students they reach than the subjects they teach.*"
- Anton Anthony, Ed. S
  Loving Education

Amazon lists 90,000 books on education. So why this one? What makes Loving Education unique?

First, this book is not about curriculum or standards or what to teach in classrooms. It's about changing how we approach education based on what modern science tells us about how human beings think, behave, and learn.

Why Loving Education?

The problem that educators, politicians, and communities face is how to get through to students of all ethnicities and economic backgrounds. My solution for all educators, regardless of the background of their students, is to build relevant relationships with students so they know the individual and not just their academic content.

This is what led my classes and schools to academic success and growth. It's not because I was the best, most knowledgeable, or most experienced teacher or principal, but because I knew all of my students. I knew they cared about me as a person and would do anything to try and be their best.

Kids are kids, regardless of their background.

I have worked in inner city schools, in rural schools, and in rich schools. I have had a student whose mother was a surgeon and a student whose mother was a prostitute.

It does not matter their background. Kids just want to know that you care. I have a dream that one day every educator would care more about the students they teach than the subject they teach.

Who I Am

My name is Anton Anthony. I received my high school diploma from Burke County High School in Waynesboro, Georgia, my Bachelor's of Arts from Fort Valley State University located in Fort Valley, Georgia, and a Master's of Arts in Teaching at Augusta State University.

Later, I obtained my Educational Specialist in Curriculum and Instruction from Georgia Regents University, and an Educational Specialist add-on in Educational Leadership from Georgia Regents University, which is now Augusta University. Augusta State University and Georgia Regents University are the same institution, but they've changed their name over the years.

In addition to my degrees, I have nearly a decade of experience in the field of education. I have worked as a classroom teacher, discipline coordinator, assistant principal, and a principal. I have worked in rural schools, poverty-stricken schools, special education schools, magnet schools, and urban general population schools.

Up until this point, my career has been a big experiment. This is the real reason why I went to so many different districts. I wanted to prove that my theories would work no matter what the environment.
The bigger my role has been in the schools where I have worked, the bigger the success rate and growth of academic achievement.

People have always asked me how I have had so much success. I couldn't explain it in a conversation. However, after examining it, this is what I can tell you: It doesn't matter the setting or the background of the students.

I have always had success with students. When students know you love them, they will do anything for you or at least try.

Goal for This Book

My goal for this book is to change the way educators, administrators, policy-makers, politicians, parents, and community members think about education. I want them to see the problem with education not as a matter of curriculum or programs or testing or the amount of money that is spent on it, but as a human problem that must be solved using an approach that recognizes the humanity of each and every student.

In this book, I will provide five key ingredients to creating an educational environment that is enjoyable, safe, and productive for everyone: love, relationships, salesmanship, creativity, and problem-solving. I will also outline my vision for an educational program that will effectively equip students to become the life-long learners they need to be in order to rise up to the challenges of tomorrow while also giving them the tools they need to become productive and engaged members of their respective communities.

CHAPTER 1: MY STORY

"It's not what you're teaching that matters. You've just got to be excited about it."
- Anton Anthony, Ed. S
Loving Education

In the introduction, I spent a little time going over my background in an effort to give you confidence that I am speaking from a position of experience, and not based on untested theory alone. However, this will help to paint a more detailed picture of who I am and why I stand where I stand when it comes to education.

As a Student

I grew up in Waynesboro, Georgia and attended Burke County public schools. Early in my educational career, I was classified as an ADHD kid and put in with the low-performing classes from 3rd through 5th grade.

I considered myself intelligent, but because of my ADHD, I made a lot of mistakes on exams and assignments. My brain was always firing with new ideas and thoughts; I was always rushing. I found myself making a lot of simple mistakes that I would catch later.

You may even see a few mistakes in this book, but as they say in church, take my mistakes for love. People always say slow down and take your time. I can promise you I am, but I lose focus very quickly. I have trained my body to be still in certain moments but my brain refuses to focus on a single thought for longer periods of time.

In elementary school, they grouped students by test scores, and since my test scores were low, I was always placed in the low-performing classes. Although I was young, I knew I wasn't in the smart class.

There were about four different groups of students, and you didn't have to be a genius to figure it out. There was the high-achieving group, the proficient-level group, the low-performing group, and the low-performing special education group. I was always in the low-performing group.

The high-achieving class was considered the smart class and it consisted of teacher's kids and a lot of Caucasian students. The proficient classes were where most kids were, but then you had my class, which was always predominantly African American with maybe one or two Caucasian students.

If they were white and in my class, you could bet your bottom dollar that they were from a poor background. Sadly, while financial status can affect the performance level of a child because it affects the resources available to them at home, early access to certain materials, and exposure to experiences, I do not believe that it affects the child's ability to learn.

I was an average student and nothing really stood out about my other teachers. But when I went to thinking about a teacher that stood out, there was one individual that was a difference maker. He was someone who had a positive influence in my educational career, as in being in school, and he meant a lot to me. He was my fifth grade teacher, Dr. Roderick Sams.

Mr. Sams was the only male teacher that I had, and he happened to be an African American. He was probably in his third year of being a teacher, but he was the first teacher to write notes on my papers like "Good job!" or "I see good in you." There was an award that he gave me called Mr. Five R.

He made all his own awards and had classroom awards. I got a couple of them, but the Mr. Five R Award was the person that was very special. It meant that you were kind of like an MVP and reminded him of himself. I wanted to be the MVP of the class, so being given that award meant a lot to me. It meant so much to me that I kept it and I kept a picture of me with the Mr. Five R award.

Mr. Sams was the reason why I was moved out of the low-performing classes. I was in a class with a rough group and he wanted me to be in another group, but I still ended up being in that similar group because I couldn't get away from the behavioral issues. But he believed in me when nobody else did, and I didn't forget that.

We took the state standardized test in the fifth grade, and I kinda got out of the low performing classes because I didn't belong there. But when I got into sixth grade, It didn't change the fact I had ADHD; of course that didn't go away. I still was active, but like I said, nothing really stood out.

Nothing really stood out about any of my other teachers. I was one of those kids who just got up and did the routine of going to school. Education was boring to me back then. I never talked to one of my assistant principals or my principals. Nobody ever really took the time to share anything with me, talk to me, or even ask me, "How are you doing?"

I had some teachers who did that, but because I was an average student and I wasn't too bad

behaviorally, and I didn't bring too much attention to myself, I went mostly unnoticed.

When I was in the sixth grade, I was a horrible reader. I hated reading all the way up
until the twelfth grade. If we ever had to read
in class, I would hide away from the teacher
so she couldn't see me, because I didn't want
to be called on to read out loud.

I wasn't the worst reader, because there were
other kids than me in that low class who read
a whole lot worse than I did. I just stuttered
over words, couldn't pronounce different
words, and other things of that nature.

I hated school. I hated it because there wasn't
anything for me to do. Nothing stood out to
me until high school, when I got involved in
sports, but I still wasn't engaged. I was still
was a B/C student.

Sports became my focus. I was involved in basketball and cross country. That's how I kind of
stood out from the crowd, because I did have a
hobby and my hobby was sports. I was athlet-
ic and I was slim and I was fast, and so that's
what made me stand out in school.

As a child, no adult really knew who I was until I got to high school and then everybody just knew I was this skinny, funny, fast kid. But that was pretty much it. I didn't realize the importance of education until I got to college.

One of the things that was missing from my educational career was I never had a chance to speak to one of my principals. I didn't even know who my principal was in elementary school because I never saw him.

Sometimes you would hear a voice on a squawk box, but you never saw the person. So I never saw him. And back then we didn't have TV, they just had the intercom system. So, you know, they'll say the announcements and then that was it.

During my K-12 years, I didn't see myself as smart. I didn't believe I would ever go to college. I wanted to be a truck driver and do some other things, all of which I did. However, when I graduated high school, my dad said I had to go somewhere.

He told me I could go into the military or I could go to college, I could go to technical school or get a job, but I had to go somewhere and move out of his house. So I chose to go to Fort Valley State University in Fort Valley,

Georgia.

Because I didn't take school seriously, I didn't have the HOPE Scholarship, which was a state-provided scholarship that covered full in-state tuition for graduating Georgia students who had at least a 3.0 GPA. That's when I realized maybe I should've focused and worked harder on my grades.

During college, I began to realize how important education was. The only loan that I had to take out in college was during that freshman year, all because I didn't get the HOPE Scholarship.

When I graduated from college, that was a big thing to me. I sent Mr. Sams an invitation and inside of that I included the picture of Mr. Five R, along with a note saying, "Thank you for believing in me."

Searching For a Purpose

I don't have an educational background. I actually have a business background. My bachelor's degree is in business management. I had this idea of starting a business. I wanted to actually start a restaurant.

I've had a lot of jobs and done a whole lot, and that's what kind of made me realize I needed to find my purpose. I did so many things prior to education, but I knew they were not for me. I cleaned floors. I was a manager at a Waffle House.

I worked at McDonald's. I worked at a plant. I worked at grocery stores. I was a manager at a workout facility. I drove transportation for Medicaid and Medicare patients. I was a real estate agent. I still am a real estate broker now, and that's what I did initially when I graduated college, because I had that business background.

I knew a whole lot, but there was something that I knew was missing. There was something that I knew that God had for me that I needed to be doing to touch lives, but I knew what I was doing wasn't it.

I would sell real estate and I would go meet my clients, show them some houses, sell the house, and get a check. But at the end of the day, I felt empty. I felt devoid and I still didn't know what it was I was supposed to be doing. But in 2009, I figured out what it was. I knew it involved teaching students.

I always enjoyed being around kids. I spent a lot of time around my family's kids and my cousins. I realized that kids always listened to me. I always formed relationships with kids just from talking and listening. I listened to everything that they talked about and I learned a lot because I learned their culture. I learned different things about the youth, what they were doing, what was cool, and what they considered old.

That was just the first thing that kind of moved me towards education. But I knew that I wanted to change the lives of youth. I knew there was something in the world that I could do that could make an impact and leave a lasting legacy.

I decided to become a recreational coach. This was the initial thing that made me want to move toward education. I started coaching basketball for a recreation department, and it was so amazing because I watched the kids look at me and learn things from everything that I did or said just as a coach.

Just from coaching, saying different things on the court, and learning different strategies about the game. They were just like, "Coach, you really know!" They looked at me like I was some type of guru, but I wasn't.

I would tell them, "I'm learning just like you. I'm learning how you play so I can coach you in the way that you need to be coached. So I'm adjusting my style to your style." Starting to coach was really that tipping point that let me know this was for me.

I decided in 2009 to get my Master of Arts in Teaching from Augusta State University. To do so, I moved back home.

I was in Atlanta and I told my wife at the time, I said, "You know what? I know this is what I'm supposed to be doing. Let's pack up, let's go back to Waynesboro, and let's live with our parents while I go and get my masters."

I left Atlanta on faith alone. We went and stayed with my mom and dad for a year while I completed my master's. Completing a master's in a year is kind of unheard of, but I completed my entire masters in eleven months, including my student teaching and everything.

My first time in the classroom, during my first semester, I had to get hours before I could start doing my student teaching. They wanted you to be around students.

It was an eighth grade class. I sat in the back of the classroom. It was about my third day. Something happened with the teacher and she had to go take a call. She told me that I was in charge.

I was nervous. I didn't know what to do or what to say. It was a social studies lesson and before she left, they were talking about share-cropping. The place that I was getting my student teaching hours was the place that I was born and raised, back home in Burke County, Waynesboro, Georgia.

I knew about the county from my grandmother, who was actually my great-grandmother. She raised my mom because my mom's mom gave her up to her grandfather's mother. So she was raised by my great-grandmother.

My great-grandmother shared some things with me when I was very young about how things were when she was growing up, and about how they obtained their land, and different things about how her dad and her family got to the point that they were. They lived in a shack on about five to ten acres. They worked for that land by sharecropping.

I got up and started reading from the text-book, but then I started giving them the real life experience. I said, "Hey, y'all know, in Burke County, there's a place called Midville, Georgia? It's a small town in Burke County, and they used to do this sharecropping that we're reading about."

I even had pictures of my grandma's house. It was a small little house, kind of like a little shack.

The kids were responding. "Yeah, I know where that road is!" Some kids actually lived on Scotts Store Road. I used those connections and tied them to the textbook so I could bring it to life for them. They were eating out of my hands. I was only with them for thirty minutes, but I said to myself, "I know this is what I'm supposed to be doing."

I went back and shared that experience with my college professors, and they couldn't believe it. They were like, "That was your first time around kids, and you taught a lesson?" I explained, "Yeah. It was an accident. She had an emergency. She left and I just took over."

That next semester I was supposed to be doing my student teaching, and my professor came to observe me. This is when I knew that this was all God.

Everyday, of course, you build relationships with your students. By the time the professor was ready to come in to observe me, I had been with the students probably four or five weeks. I was in the building and there were five other student teachers that were all completing the master's program.

She stopped by to observe me; I think I was number three of her whole roster. She was observing everyone that day because she was going to knock out the five people that were there, and then she would go back and that's how we passed. She did this three times.

I taught a lesson, and it was on religion. It was a sixth grade social studies lesson, and a part of the sixth grade social studies standards is world religions. You do the different parts of the world, including the religions that are in Asia, Europe, and Africa. I was doing the religion part, and we were studying Europe. I remember it like it was yesterday.

She was sitting in the back of the classroom and she had her mouth open. I did the lesson kind of like the Magic School Bus series. I told the kids that we were going on a trip. I said, "Everybody, put your seatbelts on. We're about to go to Europe!"

So everybody was pretending to put on their seat belts. I said, "Get ready." Every kid got ready. From whole group to small group, my professor watched as students grasped the standard content over religion. By the end of the lesson, every student got the question correct, which shocked me upon review.

Later, she told me, "Oh my God. I can't believe sixth graders were actually grasping the ideas so easily and following you."

I told her, "It's not what you're teaching that matters. You've just got to be excited about it. It doesn't even matter. Whatever you're teaching, if you're not excited about it, they're not going to be excited about it. If you don't like what you teach, they're not going to like it because it's going to be the worst lesson ever."

She said, "Mr. Anthony, I'm not just telling you this, but you have a gift. I was amazed that you had these kids eating out of your hands."

Burke County schools, where I did my student teaching, was about 60 percent African American and 40 percent Caucasian, but in my class, it was predominantly black with a few white sprinkles in the class.

She continued, "I've never seen this demographic be so attentive. You didn't have one head down. Everybody was paying attention."

I don't think they were really paying attention because of what I was saying, but I think they had so much respect for me and they just wanted to know what I was going to say or do next. I would do pretty much anything at the spur of a moment because my mind is ADHD and my brain is always firing with new ideas. If I get an idea in the midst of the lesson, I'm going to do it. That experience confirmed for me that I was on the right path. I'd found my purpose. I knew I had a calling to teach kids.

Answering The Call

When I started teaching, I started out as a sixth through eighth grade reading teacher. It was amazing. I started out the first month, and it did not have a set curriculum. I had books and an intervention program that I had to do, but otherwise, it was totally up to me.

Being creative is my strong suit. I can remember often doing an activity in my class called book in an hour. Each student was assigned one chapter of a book to read. They were the resident expert on that chapter and it was their job to explain the content to the other students. Nobody else in the class had read these books, so nobody but me knew if they were wrong or right. It took the embarrassment and shame out of reading and gave them ownership of the content.

We made the books come alive because I wanted them to understand that, yeah, we may read it, but I want it to have meaning. Then, we would make commercials for the books. My eighth grade class created videos for my sixth and seventh grade classes to help get them excited about wanting to read. I wanted them to be relevant to what we were saying and what we were doing.

So, yes, we were going to act it out. We were going to show the entire school and we wanted them to read our book. Every book that we read, we wanted the school to read it. My students were having so much fun and they were learning!

However, there was an ELA class on the seventh grade hall that was having all kinds of trouble. They hired a Spanish teacher to teach Spanish, but then changed her position to the ELA classroom. She was from a Spanish speaking country. She knew English, but didn't speak in full sentences so she was not comfortable teaching it. Every day she would come in upset and frustrated.

"I don't know. I don't know what to do. I was hired to teach Spanish. No bueno. No bueno!"

She struggled with the content and kept saying the students were bad. I talked to her a couple of times, and I knew the students that she taught because some of them were in my connections class, but they didn't behave like that in my class. I used to sometimes ask them, "Why are y'all giving that lady a hard time?"

My students would always say, "It ain't me. It ain't me. It's the other kids. They're bad down there."

One day, the students came in and started throwing crayons at her. She started crying. She quit during the day that day. She didn't even wait until the end of the day.

Over the next couple of weeks, they brought in a sub. The sub quit. They brought in another sub. Then they had a long-term sub who stayed a little bit, but I overheard the administrators talking about who they were going to put into place long term.

One of the assistant principals came to me and asked me what my certifications were. I was certified in everything because I wanted a job. He told me, "You might be going down there."

I told him, "No, I'm not going down there. I don't know anything about language arts, so I'm not going."

The next Thursday, the principal called me into the office. He said, "I need you to move. You're going. I need you to move to seventh grade language arts. I need you to clear out your classroom on Friday, because Monday you will be down there teaching."

He didn't ask me if I wanted to go. He just said I was moving. I said, "I'm not comfortable. I'm not comfortable teaching that content because I've never taught it. I'm a new teacher. This is actually my first year. Now

31

I'm moving into content that I'm not trained in teaching."

Another thing that was intimidating about taking that position was that there were veteran teachers on that hall. That Spanish teacher was the only ELA teacher that was new. Everybody else on that hall had ten plus years of experience, and they knew their content. I was intimidated. I knew I could have gotten help if I needed it, but I was very intimidated because I knew I was going into a place where my scores were going to look bad. That year, there were three other language arts teachers who were a whole lot smarter than I was.

One had five degrees, including an Ed. S. One had been teaching the same subject and the same grade for the last ten plus years. She knew her content. She could diagram a sentence. I couldn't do any of that and I still can't. She was very knowledgeable. One of the other teachers was about to retire, so he had years of experience I lacked.

I asked my principal, "Look, if I do this for you, could I please go back to my reading position at the end of the year?"

He said, "If you go down there and you are consistent with them, and you go down there and teach, I promise you I'll move you back."

I said, "Okay, sir. I'll go down and teach my heart out." At that time, my principal saw something in me that I did not see in myself. I wouldn't understand what he saw until the end of the year. I realized that I could not question administration, because he had a vision; I just couldn't see it through my eyes of a teacher. It's not until I became an administrator that I began to understand.

I was nervous. They didn't give me much transitional help besides coming in my classroom and making sure the students were orderly. Nobody showed me what I was going to be teaching. I was so country that I barely spoke in complete sentences because I was raised in an environment where you didn't have to in order to get your point across. I could communicate well enough to interview and communicate with my college peers, but the truth of the matter is when I got comfortable, I spoke just like my students.

I was very scared to teach something so unfamiliar. Although I'd passed a content test that was supposed to prove I could teach it, I was filled with doubt.

I decided on day one, I wasn't teaching anything. The first three days I just spent getting to know my kids and making sure they
knew my rules. I told them what I would tolerate and what I would not tolerate. I had
them write me an interest inventory, telling
me some things that they liked so that I could
talk about it.

On that first day, one of the kids asked me,
"What are you gonna do? Are you gonna quit
on us, too?"

"I said, no, I am not going anywhere. I'm going to be here. I'm Mr. Anthony. I'm Coach
Anthony, so I'll be here for the long haul."

I also told them that first day, "They told me
that you guys were the smartest students on
the seventh grade hall."

They didn't believe me. "They didn't tell you
that, Mr. Anthony. They didn't tell you that."

I said, "Yes, they did. I asked him to come
down here and to teach y'all because they
said that you were the smartest students. You
were just a rough group and you needed some

guidance."

I told them, "You are the smartest students in the seventh grade. You believe that?" They said, "No." I said, "I bet you by the end of this year, I'm going to prove to you that you're the smartest students on the seventh grade hall."

I started teaching that next week. I came in and I didn't know what I was teaching, but I knew from looking at the data what was probably going to end up being on the exam. I started focusing on their weak points and what I could focus on.

I did ask for help, but when we took a preliminary test after we came back from holiday break in January, the preliminary test showed that my class has one of the highest passing percentages on the hall.

They asked me what I was doing. At the time, I told them, "I don't know. I'm just teaching what I'm teaching. I don't know."

They said, "You've got to be doing something because your students are doing very well, Mr. Anthony, and this is your first year. We've got to figure out what you're doing."

They ended up splitting up the kids on the entire hallway, sending more students to my classroom for review, and I ended up teaching a lot of kids on the hallway because they thought there was something special that I was doing. All I was doing was playing games most of the time. For example, I would take a language art concept and I would start playing basketball.

You get a question and if you answer the question right, you get to shoot. You win for your team. I would say, "Everybody get ready. Give me an example of onomatopoeia and use it in a sentence," or "Create an example of a simile that you haven't heard used before." Then they would say the answer and they'd get to shoot the ball. I would also have my students create songs or raps using figurative language.

I was just doing stuff like that. I was next door to another language arts teacher, but everybody wanted to come to my class. They would tell their teacher, "Man, I don't want to be in your class. Can I go to Mr. Anthony's class?" They just wanted to see what we were doing and why we were making all that noise.

If we were reading a book, you can guarantee

and bet your bottom dollar that we were going to act it out. I have a problem with standing still because of my ADHD, and I also wanted my students to move and to be creative in everything that we did.

When we ended the year, my class had the highest pass rate on two portions of the CRCT (Criterion Referenced Competency Test): language arts and reading. Other teachers had students show tons of growth, but all of my students but one passed for each section. Considering where we started at the beginning of that year, I counted it as a major achievement.

I only had one student fail reading and one kid fail the grammar portion of the English and Language Arts (ELA) concepts. One of those kids came from the alternative school and joined us in January.

One of them did something that always touches my heart. She came to me when she got her test results and said, "Mr. Anthony, I tried so hard. I didn't want to fail."

She was crying, not because she failed, but because she thought she'd let me down. Everybody else passed, and I told the kids, "Once we pass this test we're going to have the biggest celebration in the whole world. I'm telling you, we're going to have pizza, cake, cookies, and ice cream. Everything you can ever imagine. This is going to be the best party of your life! You can tell your mommas to help."

I had parents buying stuff. I said, "We're going to shut the school down for three days. We won't have to do anything. All you have to do is just focus and prepare. Do it for Mr. Anthony; if not for yourselves, at least for Mr. Anthony.

She ended up crying and boo-hooing. I was holding her and I said, "Sweetheart, it's okay. Did you try your hardest?"

She said, "Yes, sir."

She had snot coming out of her nose and boogers and everything. She was so upset.

I said, "It's okay. That's all I really wanted you to do is try your hardest. It's all right. You did what I wanted you to do. You didn't fail both of your tests. You only failed one part of that test. I appreciate you trying your hardest. Mr. Anthony loves you for that."

The other kid that failed the reading portion

was an alternative school baby and he came to me in January. I'm pretty good, but I'm not that good. I realized that when it comes to educating kids, it's not your knowledge or your experience that matters most. It's the passion you have for the kids you're teaching that matters most.

I finished the year out with a 98.6 percent pass rate for the CRCT. I ended up getting an award, which I still have in my portfolio.

After that year, I went back to my principal who was now the superintendent. Before he accepted that superintendent position, hetold me he wanted me to stay in the classroom. He said, "Mr Anthony, I didn't expect for you to do that well with those kids. I wanted you in there because I saw some greatness in you, but I didn't expect that. I wanted them to have some consistency. I wanted them to have a stable person that wouldn't leave them because they had so many people that come in and so much instability in the early beginning of part of the year. That was my point."

I said to him, "Please, move me back to reading."

I didn't want to be back in ELA. I wanted to

be creative again. That's me. He put me back in reading, and I taught reading for another year. After that, I told him I wanted to get out and coach basketball. I said, "You know what? I think I want to be in the gym."

I asked him for a position, and he said, "Well, I have a position, but would you take it at the alternative school?"

I immediately said yes.

This was during the summer, when I was teaching summer school. I told him, "You know what? I do. I want to go. I want to go. I feel that if I could make a difference in a school like this with 900, let me go over there with the roughest of the rough and see is it me or is it them? Or whatever the case may be."

Accepting Challenges

In the midst of teaching seventh grade language arts and my connections class, I went back to school and got my educational specialist degree, but it was in curriculum and instruction. You had to get a degree in curriculum and instruction if you were going to get paid for having the degree and remain in the classroom.

Georgia did away with paying teachers for advanced degrees in educational leadership who remained in the classroom, so I decided to obtain my educational specialist in curriculum and instruction first. The degree became useful because I created my own curriculum in my reading connections class.

My next few years as a teacher, I chose to go to the alternative school. While at the alternative school, I did a little of everything. I was the PE coach, a reading teacher, and the discipline coordinator. This is where I met my mentor. At the time, I didn't know I wanted to be a principal. I thought I wanted to be a counselor.

I thought I wanted to be a counselor because I wanted to do what I was doing then and make a difference for the entire student body. I thought that counselors could do it, but then I talked to a counselor and found out they were doing so many administrative roles instead of counseling.

I said, "Well, shoot. If I'm going to go back to school, I should at least get paid for it, because they're doing administrative roles now. I'm going to go back and become a principal. I'll go back and get my administration degree. I was very blessed because the principal of that school was a man named Earl Ishmal.

Most people won't share information or try to better you. A lot of people seem to try to hide their information once they get to a position and a place in their life. They don't want anybody else to attain the position and the place where they are in life. He's the total opposite.

During one of the first conversations we had, I said to him, "Mr. Ishmal, I want to be a principal one day."

He said, "Well, you stick around me. I'll show you everything that you need to know and I'll guide you."

I enrolled in the educational administration program and started doing that. That is the reason why I became the discipline coordinator. He released it to me when I asked for duties and responsibilities. He said, "Hey, I'm going to show you what to do."

He showed me in a week and then he said, "Okay, now you have a job. If you need to come to me, ask me for what you need and I'll show you how to do it, but you have a job."

He showed me how to run a school before I was even finished with my administration degree. He has helped me more than anybody in my life. He is the reason why I have moved up so fast in the nine years that I've been in education.

Before every interview, I will call him for advice. He will tell me the things that I need to look for and questions that they may ask me. I've always walked into every interview prepared because I had that guidance and mentorship from him.

I stayed there with him for two-and-a-half years, until he got a promotion to principal of one of the larger schools in the district and left. If I hadn't accepted that challenge of coaching at the alternative school, I never would have met Mr. Ishmal and my career might have turned out very differently.

Shortly after Mr. Ishmal accepted his new position, I got my first chance to become an assistant principal at a K-5 magnet school in Columbus, Georgia. It was my opportunity to affect more lives and to find out whether or not what I'd learned from Mr. Ishmal would apply when I was on my own.

One thing that he taught me—and it stays with me to this day—is that whatever you are good at, use it to your advantage to connect with students, parents, and the community. He realized early on how unique I was and pushed me. In turn I discovered myself as a future leader. My strength as a leader is the ability to connect with people and with this gift, I set out on my first administrative duty.

The demographics for the magnet school were all over the place. The children of high-earning professionals were sitting beside the children of people who might not have even finished their middle school education, let alone gotten a high school diploma. One mother was a surgeon. Another mother was a prostitute. Despite the children's differing incomes and backgrounds, my methods were successful.

After Columbus, I accepted a position as an assistant principal at a middle school in Thomson, Georgia. I preferred working with middle school students. It was a Title I school, which meant most students that attended were below the poverty threshold and the school received federal funds. Most of the students in that school were on free and reduced lunch. But the methods I'd been using worked just as well there as they had in every other environment I'd tested them in.

My boss in Thomson was a remarkable woman, and her name was Principal Anita Cummings. I learned a lot from other people in my past, but she was the missing piece I needed to become a successful principal. She was the first person I have ever seen be so compassionate with all stakeholders.

She loved the community, loved the parents, loved her staff, and, most importantly, she loved the students. She had the warmest embrace I have ever encountered in my life. She embodies the term in loco parentis. She was the mother of every student who walked in the building. Full of love, but demanding respect from all. I never encountered a person who made people love her even more no matter how hard they tried not to like her.

One major thing she showed me was how important building positive relationships with stakeholders really was. There was one time that I had a problem with a sixth-grade student as her assistant principal. The mom was upset with the consequence I'd given that student. The parent came to the school so upset that she was cursing just as soon as she hit the door.

I attended part of the meeting with her. After meeting with her for thirty minutes, the parent walked out as happy as can be. Mrs. Cummings gave that parent a hug and held her for about ten seconds. I asked what she did to change that parent's attitude and why did she do it.

She told me that when you have a student who has to return for multiple years, you do not want parents angry at you or the school. If you make them upset, you will create an angry parent for multiple years. This can possibly affect the climate and perception of the school, especially if the parent is influential to others.

The student still was given a consequence, but Mrs. Cummings helped the mom understand why it was going to benefit the student. Mrs. Cummings taught me the importance of listening and being empathetic towards people. Although we have the power and authority to do certain things, it's not wise to use that power just because you can. Place yourself in the shoes of every person that you encounter in life so you can get a better understanding of how they feel. That was the final lesson I needed to become a successful principal.

The following year, I accepted a position as a principal at Sumter County Middle School. It was a big move for me. I had to move all the way across the state to take the position. It was also going to be a big challenge. Ninety percent of the kids were African American, and my school was located in a country town without much industry. Almost all of the kids there were below the poverty threshold.

As principal I had a lot of great days, but there were two that really stood out. I still get teary-eyed every time I think of them. The first day, I had a surprise visit from my fifth grade teacher, Dr. Roderick Sams. When I was called out of my office and saw it was him, I ran to him like he was the father I never had. I gave him the biggest embrace I have ever given a man.

He came to check on Mr. 5R. He shared with me some valuable information and ways to stay successful in administration. That visit was the best day of my life, and I'm glad that I am able to share.

I have to share with parents and educators to be mindful of what you say and speak in your students lives because we don't know how students look at you. When I was young, I looked at him like a child looks up to a superhero and on that day my superhero came to visit me. It's a day I will remember for the rest of my life.

The second day was when I was surprised yet again by Mrs. Anita Cummings and a fellow teacher. That morning, my secretary allowed Mrs. Cummings to call me on the radio. I realized it was her and I couldn't come out of my office.

I cried for at least for two minutes, but it felt like forever. By the time I made it out, she gave me her famous hug, which was an embrace that lasted for about a minute.

I couldn't help but cry, but I was embarrassed because I'm a man's man and I'm not a cry baby. Although the local newspaper had awarded me principal of the year based on a community vote, no award could have made me prouder to be a successful principal than the visits I had from Dr. Roderick Sams and Mrs. Anita Cummings.

That year was the most rewarding year of my career. I was able to make big improvements to student performance and achievement just by setting a culture and climate for learning along with making small changes in schedules.

The key to student success is getting students to believe that they can achieve, and this is how I was able to improve things at Sumter County Middle school. I was able to study the building-wide data and implement programs that improved things for teachers and students across the board.

Getting students, parents, and the community to buy into a vision is vital to the success of an educational organization, and I was able to achieve that as well. The most challenging thing during my year there, though, was being away from my own children way too much.

That's why, despite the successes and triumphs I experienced, I took a position as an assistant principal in Richmond County, Georgia. It was a step down in my career, but a step in the right direction for being a father.

Returning Home As An Assistant Principal

The most important thing for any administrator to remember is to know your role. Regardless of the title, every decision that you make should have a positive impact on students' lives.

Although I have been a successful principal, the role of an assistant principal is to support and assist in implementing the vision of the principal. The principal is responsible for the success or failure of a school, and it is his or her job to get the staff to buy into that vision.

Although I know that I am not going to stay in this role long, it feels so good to have time to be a part of my own children's education and provide them daily love and support, just as I have provided it to other parents' children throughout the state.

I have a vision for the future, though, that's bigger than being a principal. I want to be part of transforming our educational system. I want every kid to experience the positive impact of a Mr. Sams. I want every teacher to have a Mr. Ishmal in their life. This book is the beginning of making that vision a reality.

CHAPTER 2: WHAT'S REALLY MISSING FROM EDUCATION

"Everybody wants to be someone. Be that one person to every kid that walks through the door. Not just your kid, but every kid."

- Anton Anthony, Ed. S
Loving Education

The problem with our education system isn't the policies or the tools or the textbooks. It's that we've forgotten the primary purpose of an education and we've lost track of the humanity of the students. Some of our attitudes about education haven't advanced since the 1700's.

In some senses, we're still doing it the same way even though we have so many more advancements in our understanding of neuroscience and how the brain works. We really need to take a better look at what we're doing and how we're doing it.

What we're doing now is great for teaching factory workers to be factory workers, but as far as teaching people to be creative, to think on their feet, and to solve problems, it's unproductive.

Technology is changing our world so quickly that factory jobs may not even exist in twenty years. It may all be done by robots. It's important to educate our children in such a way that they can adapt to whatever future they meet if we want our society to survive going into the future.

Love

Love is the main thing missing from our schools. The problem with our education system isn't the policies or the tools or the textbooks. Think about this: Everybody wants to be someone. Be that one person to every kid that walks through the door. Not just your kid, but every kid.

Recognize students as individuals instead of just numbers. That was one of the things that made me so successful in college. I was a C student in high school, but I was an A/B student in college. I didn't go to a big university. I went to the small school of Fort Valley State University.

Our numbers in the classroom were very small. There were about fifteen to twenty-five students in the classroom. If I didn't understand something, the class was small enough to let someone know when I wasn't getting it, and to ask for the help I needed. I could ask the professors for other resources that I could go and look at that might give me a better understanding. I was successful there because I wasn't a number. I was someone.

I care about every student that walks through my doors—not just about their test scores or their pass/fail rates. I genuinely care about them, about their future, and about what they are doing with it. When you care—on a deep level—about the people you are working with and for, they will respond to it like a plant responds to sunlight.

This is where our system broke down and where it is failing not just our kids, but everyone. Maslow's Hierarchy of Needs says that love is only important once your basic needs of food, shelter, water, and sex have been met.

However, Harry Harlow's experiments with primates in the 50's and 60's proved that it does not matter how much food, shelter, water, or sex you give people; if they are deprived of love, they will not care about the rest and they will choose to die anyway.

If love is absent in the classroom, you can give your students absolutely everything else they need and you will still lose them. Too many students are being lost because they are being deprived of the most important thing: the love they need to thrive.

Relationships

Students have to trust you before they will open up to you. The problem, and the barriers that students put up, exist because they don't trust anymore.

Teachers and administrators have to work to gain that trust by building solid relationships with every student. There are four big keys to creating those relationships: consistent expectations, showing interest, asking questions, and listening to understand.

Consistent Expectations

Consistency is one of the major things that students need. The reason why students are not so successful even with behavior in class is often because the teacher and the routines are not consistent.

One day a teacher would do one thing and then the next day it would change. You have to be consistent with their learning and in the relationships that you form. Being consistent with students is what drives them to be successful.

Showing Interest

I realized that it didn't matter the color of the student or what they looked like. It didn't matter their backgrounds. I still formed relationships. I was able to form relationships because I showed interest in the student.

I can always find something to use to connect with the child and then use that connection to learn more about them. If there is something that my kids were doing outside of school that was positive,

I also made sure I was the first one there. I wanted them to know I cared about them as a person, not just a number in a grade book.

Asking Questions

I make sure I talk to my student to find out what's going on in their lives. I ask them what they did this weekend or how their day is going or how they are.

Students will tell you, especially if they trust you, if they have a bad day. They'll tell you, "I'm having a bad day," or, "My class is not going so well."

Then, you can ask them why and find out all kinds of things. That gives you a chance to solve problems before they begin.

Listening To Understand

When I talk to students, I try to listen more than I talk. This is especially true when it comes to discipline problems.

If you would just go off on that student about hitting the other student, you wouldn't even know that the child had a reason and a background story behind hitting that other student. He was at his limits.

Those are the students that get silently picked on and then go and do something crazy. They have a story. They've been picked on, but nobody ever listened to them.

I am that listening ear for my students. Because I am listening, I also find out from them where problems are happening so I can fix them and stop that same thing from happening in the future.

Salesmanship

When you're in the classroom, your customer is the student. When you're an administrator, your customer may be the teacher, the student, the parent, or a community leader.

You need to know how to identify what the major problems are that your "customer" struggles with and how your product, whether it is the education that you provide or even the students your school produces, is the solution to that problem.

You need to know what dreams the "customer" has and show them how what you're providing is the best and fastest way to get from where they are to where they want to be in life.

Creativity

Encouraging creativity is one of the big keys to getting students engaged in their education. One of the movements in education is to make sure students are self- directed learners, but we have to tap into that creative side to do that. Georgia has standards and a set curriculum we want them to learn, but in every curriculum there needs to be some type of creative opportunity.

Kids should be encouraged to create something that demonstrates they can apply what they've learned and that will allow them to express their individuality at the same time.

Problem Solving

Teach students to look at every problem as an opportunity in disguise, because if they can find a solution, they can charge people money to solve that problem for them. Help them identify their talents and then help them figure out what problem their talent can solve for somebody else.

Get them to apply the things they're learning to building a business that solves problems for other people. This will prepare students with the right mindset to meet any problem they face in the future and help them develop problem-solving skills from an early age.

CHAPTER 3. WHAT'S LOVE GOT TO DO WITH IT?

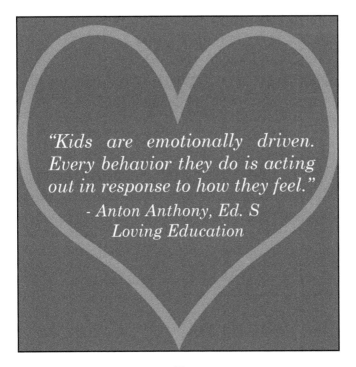

"Kids are emotionally driven. Every behavior they do is acting out in response to how they feel."
- Anton Anthony, Ed. S
Loving Education

There are those reading this who might be wondering, "What's love got to do with education?" This chapter addresses that exact question. Love is fundamental to the equation.

Love is a basic human need. If we can put love back in schools and our classrooms, if kids love education, and teachers and administrators love what you do, the environment will get better for everyone.

Maslow's Myth

"For the man who is extremely and dangerously hungry, no other interests exist but food. He dreams food, he remembers food, he thinks about food, he emotes only about food, he perceives only food and he wants only food." –Abraham Maslow[1]

Psychologist Abraham Maslow theorized that human needs existed in a kind of hierarchy. The most important needs to meet were physiological— the basic needs of survival as an individual or as a species, such as food, water, shelter, and sex. Until those needs were met, the mind simply could not focus on any other need.

This theory is taught to every educator

throughout the world during their studies on human psychology. Nearly 100 years later, though, American society and culture are proof of just how wrong Maslow was. Americans have all the food, water, shelter, and sex they can stand, but are the most medicated nation on the planet. They can buy anything, but they are miserable.

Yet nations who are impoverished and have far less than Americans do experience far higher levels of happiness in life. They are starving for food and water and shelter, but even in the midst of their struggles they find reasons for hope and reasons for happiness. Where did Maslow go wrong?

Harlow's Correction

The answer lies in primate experiments conducted by Harry Harlow in the 1950's and 60's, specifically in reaction to the widespread adoption of Maslow's theories. Because of Maslow's theories, many psychologists speculated that parenting didn't matter. As long as the child was provided with the essential needs, they would thrive.

"The position commonly held by psychologists and sociologists is quite clear: The basic mo-

tives are, for the most part, the primary drives -- particularly hunger, thirst, elimination, pain, and sex -- and all other motives, including love or affection, are derived or secondary drives. The mother is associated with the reduction of the primary drives -- particularly hunger, thirst, and pain -- and through learning, affection or love is derived" – Harry Harlow[2]

Harry Harlow believed they were wrong and that the things they were recommending would damage generations of children if left unanswered. He set out to prove it.

"...a baby monkey raised on a wire-mesh cage floor survives with difficulty, if at all, during the first five days of life. If a wire-mesh cone is introduced, the baby does better; and, if the cone is covered with terry cloth, husky, healthy, happy babies evolve. It takes more than a baby and a box to make a normal monkey." – Harry Harlow[3]

Without at least some semblance of love, something that at least felt like contact with another living being, it didn't matter how much food, water, or shelter was provided to the infant monkey. It simply didn't want to live and died for lack of that love.

"We were not surprised to discover that contact comfort was an important basic affectional or love variable, but we did not expect it to over-shadow so completely the variable of nursing; indeed; indeed, the disparity is so great as to suggest that the primary function of nursing as an affectional variable is that of insuring frequent and intimate body contact of the in-fant with the mother. Certainly, man cannot live by milk alone. Love is an emotion that does not need to be bottle- or spoon-fed, and we may be sure that there is nothing to be gained by giving lip service to love." – Harry Harlow,[4]

Our students are dying from lack of love. They are committing suicide at higher rates, join-ing gangs, engaging in promiscuous behavior, and turning to drugs or alcohol because they don't feel loved and they don't know how to get the love that they so desperately need any other way.

Love: Driving Behavior

Educators need to understand that every-thing that a student does is in some way a response to what's happening in their envi-ronment. They do not know how to tell you what hurts. Their behavior is what tells you what's hurting.

They won't know that love is what they are missing and they won't be able to say it, usually. What they will do is show it to you.

It will show up in attention-getting behaviors, in rebellion against rules, disrespect, under-performing at tasks, and a lack of motivation. Add love back into the equation, though, and suddenly those misbehaviors go away, the rebellion stops, the respect returns, and kids are motivated to perform at their best. Love is the key.

"Children who are acting in unloving ways are likely to themselves be feeling unloved, unwanted, not valuable, incapable, powerless, or hurt. (*) The response those children need isn't greater control, or bigger punishments, they need understanding, compassion, and support for their growth. LOVE." – Katie Malinski, LCSW[5]

Conversely, they will accept almost anything from someone they believe loves them. They will do anything for that person.

"I watched a young man, stand in the light rain with his son, who seemed to be about six years old. The man was engrossed in texting on his phone, completely ignoring his son who

was crying gently, plaintively telling his father that he was cold and wet and asking his dad to please pick him up and take him home. His father, without ever losing a moment's focus on his texting, reassured his son that "It's OK buddy, daddy loves you, just give me a minute to finish this and we can go home.

It reminded me of all of the times I have sat in my office as a psychotherapist and listened to people describe the stunningly bad behavior they've tolerated at the hands of other people. When they see the spontaneous horrified look on my face, they often rush in to reassure me and, perhaps themselves, that "It's OK, because I know they love me." –Avrum Weiss, Ph.D.[6]

Our need for love is so great that we will endure anything and do anything we think we need to do in order to get it. We will lie, cheat, steal, and even kill to either gain love or keep it. Kids are no different.

"Children want to please those who love them. Without a loving relationship, children have no reason to behave in acceptable ways - except to avoid punishment. It is not enough that parents love their children. That love needs to be shown and demonstrated." –Norine R. Barnes[7]

It's really crazy that we have a backwards approach to kids. We take care of their physical needs before we take care of their emotional needs. Kids are emotionally driven. Every behavior they do is acting out in response to how they feel.

If they don't feel loved, then they're not going to respond to the teacher. That is one of the most important things I really want everybody in the world to understand. It is much easier to educate kids when you provide that love.

Love and Performance

Students who have a positive, loving relationship with their teachers, who know that their teacher cares about them and the teacher makes the effort to make learning fun and awesome, are going to do everything they possibly can for that teacher. They will do for you what they won't even do for themselves.

The best person that I've ever worked for was my boss, my mentor, Earl Ishmal. He never had to tell me he was my boss. I had a level of respect for him that was so deep that anything he asked me to do, I was eager to do for him. He didn't have to say, "I'm your boss. Get it done."

He only had to tell me what he needed done. When I was done with that task, I would be eager to do more. "You need anything else, boss? Do you need for me to do anything else for you?" I would happily go above and beyond for him because of our relationship. I knew that he cared about me and loved me and wanted the best for me. If he was asking me to do it, it was because it was going to benefit the students in some way.

He never looked down on me because I was under him. Teachers sometimes tell kids, "I don't need this. I've got my education. You need this!"

Kids don't like to feel like they are being looked down on by their teacher anymore than adults do. Kids don't care about your education, and they won't care about theirs, either, until they are convinced that you care about them.

"Nobody cares how much you know until they know how much you care." – Theodore Roosevelt, 26th President of the United States of America

I've focused on providing that love in every

school and classroom where I've worked over the last nine years. It is that love which motivates my students to perform and to try their hardest. They will happily do for me what they won't yet do for themselves because they know I love them and want the best for them.

Love and Education

Every child that has some type of success. Every valedictorian, every salutatorian, they'll tell you about that one teacher that touched their hearts and inspired them to be great. Every teacher can be that teacher.

A lot of successful people can go back through their lives and say, this teacher, this one teacher, she loved me. Every teacher can be that teacher. You just have to have that love and that interest for those kids.

CHAPTER 4. BUILDING RELATIONSHIPS

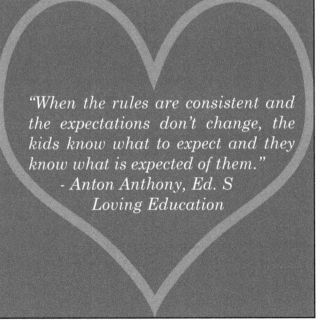

"When the rules are consistent and the expectations don't change, the kids know what to expect and they know what is expected of them."
- Anton Anthony, Ed. S
Loving Education

The key to having a successful school or classThe key to having a successful school or classroom is building positive relationships with students, parents, fellow teachers, and stakeholders. You need everybody working together for the good of the students. You can't just focus on building relationships with one group.

You can go to different colleges and universities and learn theories and methods of teaching. However, if you can't get along with the people that you interact with and you can't get them to cooperate with you, those theories and methods won't matter. Nobody is going to want to hear it. This has been a huge part of my success.

I specialize in behavior and people, whether it is with students or with adults. I study people and find ways to connect with them. I am kind of a chameleon. I can fit into any environment, because I recognize that people are people no matter their background or their status. I love my job because of the relationships that I have built with parents and students.

A lot of ineffective principals can build relationships with groups of people that are like them, but don't know how to treat the people who aren't like them. They may know how to talk, for example, to the people with the money, but don't know how to treat the people that are living in poverty. Or, they may know how to talk to people in poverty but don't know how to talk to the people who are financially well off.

Be Emotionally Aware

First, I try to be emotionally aware. If I can sense someone is angry, I don't want to address that anger by getting angry. A negative plus a negative doesn't make a positive. It just makes a stronger negative.

Building relationships is all about how you handle the people that you meet, whether those people are positive or negative. When the negative person comes into my office, my school, or my classroom, I have to be even more positive and more humble than I've ever been before in my life.

"I'm so sorry. I understand. I would be upset, too, if I were in your shoes."

Most people will calm down and work with you if they believe that you empathize with their situation and truly want to help them resolve their problem. For example, there was a special education student the other day. He was acting up and cursing at his teachers and other students. I called his mom to address the issue with her.

"I called because (student's name) was in the hallway using profanity."

She was upset.

"Well, every damn body cusses at that school."

That wasn't the response I expected, but I didn't get hostile in return.

"Well, ma'am, what we're trying to do as a school is to teach them appropriate behavior and consequences. If I have a child that just used profanity one time, I might even tell the child to call home. I would let you know he's using profanity and just ask you to speak with him when he gets home. Or I might have a repeat offender, who is always cursing or cursing at somebody, and that might be a different set of consequences."

She still didn't let up.

"You might be cussing, too, at these kids. You

know how nasty y'all are."

I kept calm.

"Ma'am , I'm not nasty. I'm here working for you. I actually work for your child so he can be safe from harm and we can make sure that nobody hurts or bullies him. Ma'am, I understand that you're upset, but I'm just trying to let you know."

She got even more upset.

"Well, it's an 'F'ing' free country. We got free speech and we can say what the 'F' we want, right?"

I didn't let her get to me.

"Yes, ma'am, you can. You can. And that's right. But, you know, he was out in the hallway. He was upset, he walked out of class, and he did this. So, this is his consequence. He's going to a timeout in school. Or, you can just come pick him up if you feel like he didn't deserve a time out."

She said, "I ain't coming."

I told her, "That's fine, ma'am. He'll be fine

where he is."
About an hour later she showed up to the school. I didn't know what to expect.

She said, "You know, I told my son to come here and misbehave. When you called me, I know I was rude to you. I just wanted to see what you were going to do and say. I apologize. I just wanted to test y'all at the school so I can call the board."

I assured her that she could expect respect even when she wasn't giving it.

"Ma'am, I wasn't going to talk to you disrespectful. I don't care if you cursed at me. I will listen to you to try to understand your frustration so I can help solve it."

Being emotionally aware can help you smooth over problems before they have a chance to become bigger problems. It can stop problems before they begin. That's why I start every day by asking kids how their evening was, or, if it's Monday, how their weekend was.

Kids will tell you. They will tell you if there was trouble at home or in the neighborhood. They will tell you if they got into a fight with so-and-so or with their parents. Then you have a chance to help them work things out before the day begins so that trouble from the night or the weekend before doesn't spill over into the day at school.

Consistent Expectations

A lot of the behavior problems that happen in classrooms are because of inconsistent teachers. One day they will feel a certain way, and the rule for that day will be that you can't talk. The next day she's letting everybody talk because she's just had it. Kids have to know what to expect, and those expectations have to be consistent.

When I was in the classroom as an ELA teacher, that's what the principal wanted. He wanted consistency. He knew that a teacher had quit and the other sub quit, so he needed someone regardless of their knowledge of the subject. He just needed somebody consistent, and the kids needed someone consistent, to be successful.

As a principal, my building-wide expectations had to be consistent and they couldn't change. I couldn't run a school where this behavior was acceptable one day and then not acceptable the other day because what message am

I sending out to parents? What message am I sending out to the students?

I couldn't run a building like that. A lot of unsuccessful teachers, principals, and leaders are unsuccessful because they're inconsistent. They do things for certain people, certain parents, certain backers and financial backers, but they won't do it for all.

You have to be consistent. When the rules are consistent and the expectations don't change, the kids know what to expect and they know what is expected of them. Parents know what to expect and how you will handle things with their kid.

Principals: Start the year with a day-one assembly that lays out the rules, the consequences for failing to follow them, and the rewards for good behavior. Don't wait until there are problems in the school. Be proactive, not reactive.

Educators: Spend the first day laying out your expectations for behavior, the consequences for not meeting those expectations, and the rewards for good behavior. Don't hold kids accountable for rules before you've taken the time to explain those rules to them, and don't get mad at kids for not following rules they didn't know existed.

Boundaries Remove The Fear Factor

When the rules aren't clear and there are no clear boundaries, it sets students and people in general up for failure. You're expecting them to read your mind and to just know what you want from them.

Imagine walking into a work environment where nobody tells you what the rules are, but they jump on your case if you break them. How safe and comfortable would you feel? You wouldn't want to work there for very long. Adults have the option of leaving a work environment like that, but students are stuck with you.

If you're driving them crazy because you don't have rules that are clear, they have no escape valve except to rebel or to stop interacting out of fear they are going to do something wrong. Neither is going to have them ready and willing to learn.

Don't Assume They Know

We can't assume that students know how to behave in school. We have to teach them what we expect of them. Every classroom teacher needs to be teaching the kids how she or he expects those students to behave in her class. The most successful teachers and principals train students in the behavior that is expected and provide rewards when the kids do things right.

A lot of kids are coming from dysfunctional and unhealthy homes. One of the common characteristics of a dysfunctional home is that there are no clear rules or boundaries. The rules change moment to moment based on how the parent feels. There is no consistency.

Teach Kids About the Different Behaviors Expected In Different Environments

II was asked to come into a teacher's class and address the students because there was a lot of use of profanity and other misbehaviors going on in that class. I told the students, "There are three different types of Mr. Anthony. There's Mr. Anthony at work. He's professional, he's dressed up, he has a suit and a tie or a bow tie. That Mr. Anthony can stand in front of a crowd of parents or students, and even my superintendent, and act, speak, and behave professionally. That's the Mr. Anthony that you guys are seeing today.

Then, there is a family Mr. Anthony. I may talk differently. I may not pronounce certain words right, because I'm with my family and I can be comfortable. I don't have to put on a facade. I can let my hair down.

Then there's a street Mr. Anthony. That Mr. Anthony is who I have to be when I am with my friends of old and I don't want them to think that I've changed because I have several college degrees. So I talk just like them, but I can't bring my Mr. Anthony of old to school and think I'm going to keep my job. I will lose my job if I talk like I do when I'm with them on the weekend or at a club in Miami.

There's a school behavior that's expected of you. Your school behavior does not include using profanity. It does not include playing and picking at folks and bullying and being mean. That is not school behavior. Now, I'm not going to punish you until I tell you it's not right. So now that I've told you, if you get sent to my office, you can go ahead and tell your parents that Mr. Anthony said that this is your warning.

From now on, If I get you in my office, there will be no more talking because I gave you a warning. Now that's my stern Mr. Anthony. I want you to know that I mean business because at the end of the day, I don't want to assume that you know certain behaviors."

Students of today are not being taught at home about appropriate behaviors for school. Half of parents don't know or understand the appropriate behaviors themselves. If only you could be a fly on the walls when parents come into the schools. I have learned so much about student behavior when I speak with their parents. Sometimes students are a direct reflection of the environment they grow up in.

Rules Without Relationships = Rebellion

When a kid who grew up in a dysfunctional environment is introduced to an environment where there are clear and healthy boundaries, you have to expect them to test those rules and boundaries. They want to see if you mean what you say.

Until they trust you, they are going to see

those rules and boundaries as restrictions on their freedom. That's why it's important to be consistent and to help them understand why you put the rules into place that you've put into place.

Showing Interest

Building relationships with kids starts with showing interest in them. You can't expect them to be interested in you. You have to be interested in them and learn more about them. It's the interest in them that will open them up to you.

I worked with this one student at the alternative school, a Caucasian male.. He was the biggest eighth grader I've probably ever seen in my life. He never spoke to anyone.

If you spoke to him, he would just nod. He sat by himself at lunch. Nobody talked to him. If you said something to him, he would say yes sir or no. And that was it.

He came to the alternative school because he was in credit recovery. His grades were bad in the other school because he was going through some personal things. He was going through so much with his mom and dad, his grandparents were raising him and were his guardians.

I noticed him because I related to everybody but him. At the time, I was the coach at the school and everyone had to go to my class at some point. He was a student that nobody talked to, but I decided that I wanted to get to know him.

One day at lunch, I went over to him and asked him various questions about things he liked. It turned out he was a big Clint Eastwood fan. He told me about a boxed DVD set he had, with four or five different Clint Eastwood movies.

I said, "I don't know about Clint Eastwood but I would like to know."

He was skeptical. "You sure? You really do?

I said, "Yeah, I would like to know."

The next day, he brought me the set of Clint Eastwood movies. That weekend, I went and watched it. That following Monday I came back and said, "Hey, I watched Dirty Harry and it was really good."

During lunch that day we discussed the details of the movie and everybody watched as He and I conversed at lunch. People asked what we were talking about, and I told them it was a secret or they wouldn't understand so they wouldn't bother him about it.

He and I talked about all the other Clint Eastwood movies and what he thought about them. He told me about visiting some type of park where he saw Clint Eastwood's Hollywood Star. Over the next couple of days, Travis told me about all of his favorite interests and music. He even shared with me about where he lived and how his granddad collected firearms.

He must have gone home and told his granddad that we talked, because one day when his granddad came and picked him up he invited me over to his house.

I ended up going to their house several times and I had the time of my life. The student and I rode four wheelers over about a hundred acres. They had a gun range where I shot rifles and my personal firearm, and I mean it was a time he and I talk about to this very day.

Just those few instances of showing interest in the student as a person resulted in building a life-long relationship that continues to this day. Because of the student, I didn't have any discipline problems in my classes at the alternative school. He was quiet and would listen to the other students and alert me to problems before they could happen.

Going Beyond the Classroom

When the students have sporting events such as recreational games and middle school events, I'm there. Not as just a teacher or as an administrator but as a supporter. I did it as a principal and I do it now.

It wasn't a part of my school duty. I did it just to watch them and support their interests and what they were involved in outside of school. If they're doing something positive, I want to spend time with them and let them know that they are important.

I wanted them to feel like they are part of my family, especially if they're a part of the school where I work. I want them to get the message, "You are important."

Every child is important. If you invite me, I

don't care what it is, I'm going to be there if it is possible for me to be there.

My Facebook page is full of posts from where I was out there showing support to my students of every school I have ever worked. It doesn't matter if it is basketball, football, cheerleading competitions, softball, baseball, or tennis matches.

It doesn't matter if it is a boy or a girl, I treat it all the same because I want them to understand that their teacher, principal, or assistant principal has their back.

Connecting with Parents

Parents want to be part of their kids' education. They want to support their kids, but they often don't know how.

I just had a grandparent come in and she told me, "Mr. Anthony, we don't know how to do this stuff. I was telling my husband, I don't know how to do this math."

One of the children in the school where I worked was in the special education program and she was given a worksheet to do. It was on translating a line on a graph. I am far from a math teacher, but the task was simple. They had a line and then the directions were to move the line to the right five times. You had to count one, two, three, four, and then make that same parallel line on fifth line. Or they had to move left five..

The student was frustrated because she didn't know how to do the math. While in class she said, "I don't know how to do this s~~~!" and then threw the paper and her pencil on the floor.

The student had a valid point. She had already complained that she didn't know how to do it and was showing her frustration in the classroom, but she didn't know how to express it properly, so that was her way of communicating her frustration. I went down to the classroom and got the little girl out of class because she was being disruptive.

I told her the appropriate thing to do. I said, "Sweetheart, we're in here and we're here to help you. But you have to first attempt to do the work. If you don't know how to do anything, put it on paper and then show us you don't know how to do it, then we'll know how to help you. But we can't help you without you at least trying to do it."

I also told her, "That's not school talk. We

don't talk like that at school. If you do that at home, I'm not telling you it's fine, but you just don't do that here."

So she understood that she should've done something, and she understood that what she said was wrong, because she went to boohoo crying before we called Grandma, because that's who she was staying with at that time. Grandma came up right then and was at the school within fifteen minutes.

She told me, "This is the same sheet that she had at the house, and we didn't know how to do it."

I told the grandmother, "Sit down, I'll teach you right now."

I showed her and we did three problems together. She said, "Oh my God. That helped me out so much. Now I know how to do it."

She told the girl, "Come here, baby, I can show you how to do it now."

I said, "Yes, she can."

Once I helped the grandmother, it was like a light went off in her head and she was able to help the child right then and knew how to help her at home. Parents need to know that we're here to help. We need to offer them whatever resources or assistance they need. A lot of these parents didn't finish school themselves. In eighth grade, this girl was doing algebra. Her grandparents may have never even taken a single algebra class.

It's a huge mistake to assume that the parents know as much as the teachers do or can help the kids at home. A lot of those parents haven't been college-educated and don't know what you know. They may not have even finished high school, and then you're asking them to teach this stuff to their kids at home.

Also, don't let the only time the parent hears from you be the times when you are having problems with their kid. Parents don't want to hear about your problems with their kid. They want to hear your solutions for the problems their kids are experiencing. They want to hear what their kid did right, as well.

When parents know that you are on their kid's side, and that you are on their side, they will cooperate with you and want to support you in the work that you do. I told parents I wanted them to be a part of our school and to come in any day because I'm not going to put on a dog and pony show. I need your help to make this school be even better.

Connecting with the Community

Great school districts have great parents, but they also have great educators that care and community members who work with them. When those three pieces come together and work together, they have success. It doesn't matter about the income of the area. If communities and families and schools are together and working as one, so that no matter where students go, they can get the help they need, the educational system will succeed.

As a principal and an educator, I take time to get involved in the community and to make the community part of the educational experience. Attend local churches of your students, eat at local restaurants of parents, take flyers in the community detailing the great things that you have going on in your classroom and school. I went out of my way to reach out to church leaders, community organizations, and business owners because those are the people who will be living with the results of the schools we create for them.

If you look at a lot of the most successful high school sports programs, they create this culture around their sports program. They work to get the support of parents, they have the support of the school, and they also reach out and get the support of the community. Those programs are successful every year.

It doesn't matter. Ten years down the road, they are still going to be successful because the community is together, the school is together, the parents are together, and the kids have the support they need to succeed. If you want move a school academically, it has to be the same exact way.

Unfortunately, some school districts take the focus off of the students, off of the family, off of the school, off of the community. Those same schools only focus on curriculum and new programs to buy and then they wonder why their students keep failing. The students aren't getting the supports they need and that support may need to come from one of the above.

Positive Climates Create Positive Results

"As defined by the WestEd study, a positive school climate includes caring relationships

between teachers and students, physical and emotional safety, and academic and emotional supports that help students succeed. The goal of a positive school climate is "a sense of belonging, competence and autonomy" for both students and staff" –Jane Meredith Adams[8]

If we're expecting to see good behavior out of kids, we need to be doing the things that help them behave well. That begins with changing the climate of the school for kids and the perception of the school for parents and community members.

The climate of a school directly affects the academic achievement of the students in that school. When the climate of a school is positive, there is a direct impact on academic achievement. Research shows that the better the climate of a school, the higher the academic achievement of the students.

The State of Georgia recently adopted PBIS (Positive Behavior Interventions and Supports) in schools because they realized how important a school's climate was to helping students get the most of their education. It's true for classrooms, too. The better the climate for learning, the greater the student achievements will be for those teachers.

Changing the climate of the school begins before students step foot in the building. As educators, we compare scores to other schools and to other teachers. What we don't often do, though, is compare the climate of the schools and teachers to one another.

Changing the climate comes first. When the climate is positive, the students are ready for learning. For administrators, the changes to the climate must be building-wide and present in all classrooms to improve student achievement.

Think about it: If you have a spouse and you want to do something romantic, you have to plan something special and set the mood for the evening. Whether it's a candle-lit dinner or a picnic in the park, you have to make sure the setting is just right. Setting the mood for your building is the same.

As principal, I spent my summer planning to create order and making the environment conducive to learning so that on day one, I could set the right tone and mood for learning. That strategy proved to be successful.

The perception of a school directly affects the

level of support received from parents and community members. If you want students to perform their best, it begins with changing the climate and creating that positive perception of your school.

I invited parents and community members to be part of the school. I worked with parents to be sure that they understood that I was working for them and I was on their side. I wanted them to know that I was doing my best to support their student so their child could achieve their best.

One of the things I did as principal was hold a school-wide talent show for those middle schoolers very early in the school year. I wanted to identify the kids with hidden talents so we could support them and encourage them throughout the year. I did it early so that parents and teachers wouldn't worry about grades yet. They could just enjoy watching their child perform.

The talent show drew in parents that normally wouldn't have set foot in the school, just so they could see their child on stage. This gave me a chance to talk with them and start building the relationship with them so I could earn their trust. This way, I could gain their confidence that I was sincerely interested in helping their child achieve their best. It also drew in community members who wanted to see what our school was doing for their neighborhood.

CHAPTER 5. SELLING EDUCATION

"We expect kids to get why they should need what we're selling when we don't even know why we're selling it. How can we expect them to buy a product we don't understand?"
- Anton Anthony, Ed. S
Loving Education

The teacher must be a salesperson. They have to be good at selling the curriculum to the students, but they're not trained to do that. They don't know how to sell it to the students and they don't know how to do marketing because they don't know how to put themselves in the students' position.

They need to learn to say, "OK, the student's not buying this. Why? Why aren't they buying? What can I do to get them to buy it? I know what the product does, but does the student know what the product does?"

If you can't market your program, if you can't sell it, and if you can't follow up and give the customer service that the kid needs, you're going to fail in the classroom and you're going to fail as a school.

Understanding Your Product

One of the many jobs I worked before I entered the educational field was real estate. I sold houses for a living. As a salesperson, if you can't explain to the customer what your product does and why it is needed, you aren't going to be able to sell it. It's that simple.

Unfortunately, our teacher education pro-

grams aren't teaching salesmanship anymore. Eighty percent of teachers and administrators probably have no idea why we teach
what we teach or do what we do, and what the
point is of even following the different things
that we follow.

We expect kids to get why they should need
what we're selling when we don't even know
why we're selling it. How can we expect them
to buy a product we don't understand? That's
not fair to them. It's not respectful of their
time.

All that kids have of value is their time, and
we are forcing them to trade it to us in ex-
change for their education when we can't explain to them what it's going to do for them or
why they need it. No wonder they rebel and
reject it.

A friend of mine and I were discussing this
the other day. She was telling me about the
struggles she'd had with her son when he was
in school. This is what she told me.

"I fought my son tooth and nail every single year from kindergarten through seventh
grade trying to get him to want the education
that he was being given. NOTHING helped.

He didn't care about a career—he was too young to understand why it mattered. He didn't want to be forced to sit in a classroom or guilt-tripped into being there. He kept asking why he needed an education and I had no answers to give him that made sense to him.

Then came seventh grade. I told him at the beginning of the year: This one is on you. You will pass or you will fail. It is up to you. I am not fighting you. I am not going to be on top of you. I am going to let you choose your future. I chose seventh grade because I knew it wouldn't go on his permanent record and the consequences would be real but not too hard a burden to bear. Three weeks before the end of the school year he is failing math, science, and English—his best subjects.

I turned to God almighty for help. I tell Him, 'Lord, give me the answers I need, because I think I'm going to kill this kid.'

The issue, God showed me, was control. My son did not want to be controlled—and he was proving to us that we could force him to attend school, we could force him to sit in a classroom, we could force him to do work—but we could not force him to turn that work in. We could not force him to perform.

That day, it occurred to me for the first time to ask the most important question of all. Why do we teach the subjects we teach? This was not a question anyone brought up during my two years of training in education or during the years I'd spent in school before that. And the answers came with the question.

Education is nothing more than a tool box that one generation passes on to the next, and everything inside that toolbox is designed to help them find and evaluate the answers to their own questions about life, the universe, and their particular place in it.

It is not about adults controlling children but about giving children the tools they need to control themselves, to find and live their purpose, and to discover how to think through the inevitable problems that face them in life so that they can turn any problem into an opportunity that benefits them rather than works against them. We are meant to be teaching children how to think, not what to think.

We teach reading, writing, speaking, and foreign languages because 99 percent of the questions a child has about life, the universe, and their place in it have already been answered by someone else. Those things give them the tools to cross time, space, and cultural barriers to find the answers they need.

We teach science because it puts in their hands the ability to test those answers to be sure they are true. Great lies are 99 percent truth. You must test them repeatedly in order to find the lie within them. We teach math because it is the language of relationships—it is universally true stories about relationships that apply no matter when or where they are.

We teach history because it is a compilation of all the experiments that humanity has conducted in how to live and the results they got with those experiments so that we do not need to repeat the mistakes and can capitalize on the successes.

We teach art so that we will begin to understand just how limited an individual perspective is and how important it is to gain multiple perspectives in order to find the truth about any given topic. It teaches us that what we see from where we stand is NOT the truth but is in fact a very limited, distorted view of the truth.

We teach music because music is the native

tongue of love and all beings need love. It is a universal communication system and all things in our universe respond to it. We teach dance because dance happens to be the body's natural response to music.

We teach health because it is important to know and to understand how to care for the body that you've been given, as what the body needs is your first clue to what the rest of you needs—heart, mind, and soul.

We teach philosophy because it is the study of how to think. It gets you to challenge your assumptions, ask the right questions, and seek the answers. If you don't ask the right questions, don't be surprised if your answers about life are all wrong.

We teach government because it doesn't matter how many rights you have if you don't know what they are or how to speak up for them. It's that simple. Children need to be taught what their rights are, how those rights can be defended, and why those rights matter in the first place.

We teach economics because knowing how to manage, protect, and grow your money is an important step in teaching kids how to manage, protect, and grow any resource they have.

We used to teach religion, but we threw it out because we did not understand its value. Religion is the study of rules for relationships, which is why it has survived through every culture and creed. Any society that removes religion begins to crumble and fall apart because the relationships that bind people together begin to crumble. That's what is happening today."

I asked her if I could put this in my book because it was just such a beautiful explanation. She said I was more than welcome to use it.

Explaining the Benefits

If you can't explain the benefits of an education to the kids in a way that they can understand, why would you expect them to want to be there in that classroom? Even adults don't want to be forced to take classes when they can't see their benefit.

A friend of mine is a perfect example of this. She took geology class in college. She dropped out after just three weeks. When I asked her why she dropped the class, she explained, "I don't care about rocks. I don't care how rocks are formed. I don't want to know about rocks. It doesn't matter to me. It's not going to impact my life."

Three years later, though, when she was looking to make jewelry, guess who wished she hadn't dropped out of her geology class? Now knowing how rocks were made was important to her because that's how gems and precious metals are made and that is how you learn to detect them in their rough state. Rough gems and precious metals don't look anything like the pretty ones in the jewelry store. If somebody had made it relevant to her life and demonstrated the benefits to her, she wouldn't have dropped out of the class.

Make learning relevant to the kids. If you don't make that learning relevant, students won't respect the content. They also won't respect you for not even selling it. If you're not making it relevant to them, they are not going to respect you or respect what you teach. I deal with this every day.

Teachers just don't understand it, and I don't want to hurt their feelings. I try to tell them in a nutshell, "What are you doing in the classroom to support the kids and make it real for them?"

Most of these kids are living in urban areas. Some of them have never been to the beach. They didn't understand what weathering is.(Don't worry if you don't know what this is. Weathering is the breaking down of rocks, soil, and minerals as well as wood and artificial materials through contact with the Earth's atmosphere, water, and biological organisms.)

They don't understand the science content. This is where teachers need to put in the effort to make it real for those students. That's why we have to use field trips.

Respected author and educator Ron Clark talks about this in his books. Before his students went on any field trip, he had them do hard research and he created an assignment about the place they were visiting. Once the students arrived at the location, they knew the information and they understood the reason why they studied the material. The field trip just made it real for them.

We have to provide that relevance in the curriculum because otherwise it's just a couple of pages in a book and a couple of standards on the board. They don't see how it's going to apply to their life outside of the classroom.

For example, I saw this on YouTube. A guy took Shakespeare and presented it as if it happened in 2015. The guy was translating what Shakespeare was saying into street language, like, "Bro, how could you do that? This is my love of my life!"
He took the way Shakespeare wrote it and presented it in the same way they talk in the neighborhood. The student not only were able to understand what was going on, but they remembered it like it was the back of their hands. He took something that took place a long time ago and showed them how it was still relevant to their lives today. That's what needs to happen.

If you can take any content and make it real for them, they will remember. If you present Shakespeare as Shakespeare, they're not going to remember it. It's going to be the most boring thing in the world to them because they're going to struggle to understand the language.

However, if you can show them Shakespeare in a way that they understand, they'll see how relevant it is. Everybody's been in love or thinks that they've been in love. If you can relate that to students, it will stick with them for a lifetime.

Knowing Your Audience

This goes back to building relationships. Know what the kids in your class want out of life. Know what their interests are. Help them to understand how the subject you are teaching is going to help them get where they want to be in life. Use their interests to help make it fun, engaging, and relevant to their current life.

You can't use the same techniques to teach pre-kindergarteners that you use on high schoolers. It's important to know your audience, know what their needs and interests are, and put your lessons together based on that information. "Itsy Bitsy Spider," for example, works great on the pre-K and kindergarten classes, but it doesn't work well for junior high and high school kids.

If your kids like rap music, use that interest to encourage them to create raps about the subject you are teaching. Whatever they are into, use that in your lesson planning.

Tracking (and Demonstrating) Results

Students need to see the progress they are making just as much as adults do. They need feedback from teachers to know where they are, and they need positive feedback more than they need negative feedback.

Algebra tells us that if you add a negative to a positive, you get no growth. You're left with potential and nothing else. If you want to see positive growth after encountering a negative, you have to add twice as much positive as you have negative to get there.

This is true for every human being and every situation. You can't get positive growth out of a kid by heaping constant negative on him or her. You're only going to get more negative.

At the beginning of the year, find out where kids are and give them a fun way to visualize their progress based on their interests. For example, if a kid is into racing, have them create a car with their name on it and make a progress chart. Every time they make positive progress forward, move their car closer to the finish line.

If the kid is into music, have them create a microphone or an album and make a "world tour" progress chart. Every time they make progress, they get to move their microphone to the next location on their imaginary world tour. This can encourage them and help them develop intrinsic motivation to see themselves cross that finish line or make all the stops on their tour.

Building Trust

Consistency is the first part of building trust, because it lets students know what to expect, but beyond that, you need to be sure that they know you believe in them, want them to succeed, and genuinely care about them.

We have to be that person they can talk to, that safe place in their lives, and then they can learn. Once they know that they're in that safe place, it's like their minds open up and they're able to learn.

Students will block their minds when they don't feel safe. It's not to say that they can't learn, but they'll block out what you're saying until they feel that they can trust this person because they know that she or he has their best interests at heart.

It doesn't matter what the content is. Students just want to know that they are safe and that you care.

Take Them Seriously

When students have problems, take them as seriously as you want your own problems to be taken. Sometimes adults can have a tendency to act like students are being overly dramatic about their problems because, in the adult's eyes, the adult's problems are bigger than that.

To the student,though, that is the biggest problem of their life. They need to know that you take that problem seriously and that you are willing to listen and to help them with it.

Be Understanding

If a child makes a mistake or gets into trouble, address the problem, but don't yell or fuss at them. Let them know that we all make mistakes and we all do the wrong thing sometimes, but we just need to do our best not to repeat the mistake and not to do that wrong thing again.

When they see that you aren't going to yell or fuss at them for their mistakes or for giving into their temptations, they are more likely to come running to you with their problems rather than hiding them away out of fear that you'll be disappointed with them.

I have several kids in my building who are troublemakers, but I've worked to build that trust with them. It's so amazing to watch them run to me now to tell me when they are about to get in trouble. These are kids who never run to anyone. That response, though, comes from building trust with them.

Believe In Them

There are no bad kids. There are bad behaviors. Some teachers write kids off as "bad kids" because they misbehave. They don't want those kids in their class.

The truth is, those "bad kids" are the kids with the most potential. They are the future leaders of society. Most of them have been through more than you will ever know and they are doing the best they can to deal with situations that many adults wouldn't handle as well as they are.

Believe that every kid in your class is capable of greatness, and then challenge them to become what you believe they can be. Nobody can believe in themselves until someone outside of them believes in them. Show them the great person you want them to become by how you speak to them, think about them, and treat them.

That class of seventh grade ELA students that I inherited was labeled as "bad." They weren't bad kids, though. They were kids with a lot of potential that nobody had tapped into yet. They were smart kids, but they didn't believe it until I believed it for them and showed them I believed in them by telling them they could do things nobody else thought they could do.

Be Excited About Your Product

I told all my teachers and student teachers, back when I was in the classroom, that I don't care if we teach the same lesson. My lesson is going to be way better than yours because I'm going to sell it. I'm going to put my heart into it and I'm going to put my personality into it.

Everyday when my kids walked into class, I said, "Y'all, I can't wait to teach y'all this lesson today because it's amazing. They were like, "What? What is it about? What is it about?"

"You'll learn when we get started."

My enthusiasm and excitement about the lesson meant they were paying attention just to see what I was going to do. Then they'd go to the next class and they'd tell those kids, "Oh, Mr. Anthony is going to do this."

The next class would come in and say, "Mr. Anthony, we heard what you are going to do."

The thing was, I might not do it in that class. I might have had a better idea of what to do for the next class. I didn't know for sure what I was going to do. So the kids would come in eager to see what was going to happen just from the buzz they'd heard from the class before them.

It was easy for me to be enthusiastic about my lessons because I love the interaction with students when they're actually learning. I love watching when the light bulb finally goes off for them on a concept that they were struggling with and they say, "Oh, okay. I think I got it!"

If you aren't excited about teaching your lesson, why should kids be excited to learn it? If you aren't excited about the subject, the kids won't be either.

Securing the Commitment

Money is a metric for two things: the amount of trust you've earned from your prospect that you can deliver a result they desire, and the amount of commitment your prospect has to getting that result.

If you don't have a tooth ache, it doesn't matter how trustworthy your dentist is, you are not going to pay them anything because you have no commitment to getting that tooth fixed. You don't need that service.

If you have an abscessed tooth, though, you will happily pay that dentist whatever he asks to fix that tooth because you have a supreme commitment to ending the pain you are experiencing.

However, that's only true if you trust the dentist. If that dentist has a horrible reputation for leaving people worse than they were when they came into his office, you will look for anyone but him to help you with your tooth.

Once you've earned the trust, you're ready to secure a commitment from your students. No sale is made until your prospect has secured their commitment to getting the results you're promising you can deliver by paying the money. Your kids aren't going to pay you in money. They are paying you in their time.

After you've helped them understand the product and explained its benefits, you have to get the commitment from them by asking for it. Ask them to commit to doing their best, to learning as much as they can, and to working as hard as possible to getting the results you're promising them you can deliver. Get them to take ownership of their learning.

If you're an administrator, you need to present your vision to your teachers, to your parents, to your students, and to the community and get each group to commit to helping you make that vision a reality. You need to understand that for community members, the product you are producing is the students.

Without the commitment from the community, you are going to struggle to produce the high-quality product that will help secure the future of that community and bring in the tax dollars that come from productive citizens. It's in their best interest to help you because educated consumers not only make more money and have more money to spend, but also are less likely to cause problems.

CHAPTER 6. BRINGING CREATIVITY (AND FUN!) TO THE CLASSROOM

> *"Play, because it is both spontaneous and fun, creates an uninhibited environment for students to practice the things they are learning without the fear of failure."*
>
> *- Anton Anthony, Ed. S*
> *Loving Education*

Creativity and fun are extremely important in getting kids to learn. In fact, they are important for learners of any age. Our brains are wired for both, and both have a huge role to play in keeping people engaged and interested, especially when it comes to learning.

However, until kids trust you, they aren't ready to be creative. That's why I put the chapter on selling education ahead of this one. When students trust you, they won't be afraid to take risks. In order to really be truly creative, you have to know that if you fail, you're not going to be judged. They have to know that it's OK to fail and it's OK to not get things right.

When I was in the classroom, I did an activity with my kids one day. They were using bendy straws, and they had to put a ball on top and balance the weight. The most important part of it, was learning to use their minds to create a solution to the problem. I allowed them to create different things because I wanted them to know that every idea that they were going to come up with was not going to be right.

The thing might fall over, but instead of giving up, I wanted them to use that failure and learn from it. If they had two legs and it was leaning one direction, maybe they needed to add a third leg and make it a tripod.

I use activities like that just so they will not be afraid to take risks. When you're not afraid to take risks is when the best products are created. Successful individuals create their best work once they're allowed to be creative and stop being afraid of the risks or of what people may say about them.

The Role of Creativity In Memory

The right side of the brain is where the subconscious mind is located. The subconscious is in charge of storing all of our memories and it is also in charge of our creativity.

"LTM (long-term memory) is stored and retrieved by association. This is why you can remember what you went upstairs for if you go back to the room where you first thought about it." -Saul McLeod[9]

Long-term memories are stored based on their relationship to things we already know and have encountered. If the brain can't immediately find a connection between a new piece of information and something you already know, it tosses that information in the brain's equivalent of a junk drawer and stores it for later processing.

"During sleep, when attention to sensory input is at a minimum, the mind continues to process information, using memory fragments to create the images, thoughts, and narratives that we commonly call "dreaming". Far from being a random or meaningless distraction, spontaneous cognition during states of sleep and resting wakefulness appears to serve important functions related to processing past memories and planning for the future." - Erin J. Wamsley, Ph.D. and Robert Stickgold, Ph.D.[10]

The later processing happens during times when we are dreaming, day dreaming, or our brain is doing some task that doesn't require a lot of brain power like gardening, driving, or showering.

This is why so many inspirations come from dreams, daydreams, and in the shower. That's when the brain has the chance to spot connections between things that might not seem related at all.

Creativity gives the brain a chance to play with the new information it's received and put it into practice mentally, to try different things, and to test out ideas. The more that the brain uses this new information, the more connections it forges with information we already know, and the easier it becomes to remember that new information later.

"The brain, it seems, does not make much of a distinction between reading about an experience and encountering it in real life; in each case, the same neurological regions are stimulated." - Annie Paul Murphy[11]

One interesting thing that neuroscientists have discovered is that the subconscious mind doesn't distinguish between things that really happen to you and things that you vividly imagine happening to you. It experiences those things and processes them as if they actually happened. They discovered this phenomenon when they were monitoring people who were reading fiction.

The more sensory information that was provided to the reader, the more vividly the scene was experienced in the brain. So, if you want to make it easier for your students to remember a piece of information, have them get creative with it!

The Importance of Play In Learning

"But is war an art so easily acquired that a man may be a warrior who is also a husbandman, or shoemaker, or other artisan; although no one in the world would be a good dice or draught player who merely took up the game as a recreation, and had not from his earliest years devoted himself to this and nothing else?" -Plato[12]

Play, because it is both spontaneous and fun, creates an uninhibited environment for students to practice the things they are learning without the fear of failure. The pleasurable nature of play encourages children to continue trying even when they don't succeed the first time or the first hundred times.

If you watch children playing video games, they may fail to complete a level one hundred times, but because they are having fun, they won't quit trying to complete it until they succeed. They know that the game is built to ensure they can succeed, so they keep trying even when they are frustrated or discouraged.

Additionally, because play releases endorphins, which are the feel-good hormones, into the bloodstream, play creates positive associations with the content the student is learning. During play, more parts of the brain are being activated and this helps with their ability to remember and recall the information they are learning. Simply put, if you want students to enjoy learning and learn faster, make a game of it.

Encouraging Student Ownership of Learning

Let kids take responsibility for their own education. Right now, most school districts teach like we've always taught. The teacher is at the front of the classroom and they are the subject matter expert. It's their responsibility to pass on the knowledge to the students. The student is only responsible for regurgitating what the teacher teaches.

We need to change that. Kids need to be responsible for their own education. We can't give it to them. They need to be responsible for it. The only way they will grow up and want to do better is when we're not handing it to them. The more you work for something, the more you covet it.

That's why I like working for my money and I don't like to be given money because I will lose the value of money. That's why I have to have my kids do something for money. It's because otherwise, they won't understand the value of it. If you don't understand how hard someone worked for this, then you will spend it without a care in the world because you are not the one working for it.

I want kids to work for their education just their like their parents work on a job. One of the things I do is have the students teach certain things. That builds the students' confidence when they are able to share different things about a topic that they know.

One day at school, we had a career awareness class and it is usually taught by our counselors, but neither one of them was there. I covered the class and I asked the students what they wanted to do in life. I asked all the students to tell me three different things that they wanted to be in life, and I used that data to divide them up into different groups.

Each group had to do research on the information about the career they chose. Then, the group was required to teach that information to the other students. This class was a pretty large class with about fifty kids in it.

I told them it was OK that they didn't know certain things. That's why I put them in groups. Other people in their group knew more about the career because some of their parents were, for example, truck drivers. I had a couple of kids that wanted to be You-Tubers and certain kids knew different information about being on social media.

One of the things that they had to know was how many years of college was required in order to go into that career. I was amazed by the sixth graders and how much information that they knew.

I told them it was OK if they didn't know certain things. I wanted them to research and find out. They took out their phones because we were in our auditorium and didn't have any computers to use. They loved it.

They loved being able to research different things that they didn't know. They loved being able to teach the other kids. I called them experts now that they had researched and knew different information. I used to do this in my classes. I would have students pick a topic that they liked and then research information on that topic.

Because they were my experts, no one in the class could really tell them more about the topic than they knew. They were confident in sharing what they'd learned, because they really wanted to do that.

The kids who were listening to the presentations were impressed. They didn't know the information they were learning. For example, I didn't know that a lot of people make money off of YouTube. There are people that get checks for $15,000 or $20,000 a month off of YouTube. Some kids were like, "I didn't know that! I want to be a YouTuber." Now that they have that information, though, it may expose them to new things and career paths that they might want to explore.

Engaging Students and Demonstrating Value

When you have students apply their creativity to solving problems, you demonstrate the value of what you've just learned. You don't have to tell them how they can use this in the real world, because you are showing them. Not only are they having fun, but they are seeing how the information they've just learned applies to their life and helps them.

A friend of mine had a history teacher in the tenth grade who wanted students to see that history wasn't just something that happened to other people. She wanted the students to see how it directly impacted their lives and their families, so she assigned them a family history research project.

My friend was a little scared of this project because her parents were divorced and her mom wasn't talking to her dad's side of the family. Her mom's parents were divorced, too, and her grandma wasn't in contact with her grandpa's side of the family, either. But she decided to give it a try.

At the end of the lesson, she was able to see how, for example, the completion of the transcontinental railroad moved her family from Indiana to California. She was also able to see how World War I and World War II had changed things for their family and caused them to move again. She could track how the Great Depression had forced the family to sell their land in order to make it and how the family had fallen into poverty as a result.

While the assignment wasn't easy for her to complete, the rewards were well worth the effort. History wasn't something that happened to other people. It was now something that directly impacted her life.

Providing Opportunities for Concept Application

One of the things that I did with my reading classes, as I mentioned earlier, was have them create commercials for the books we'd read. We would record video commercials to entice other classes to want to read those books. This was one way we applied the concepts we learned by reading the books to real life problems.

Another way to provide opportunities for concept application is to put the kids who are ahead in class to work tutoring those kids who are behind or who haven't quite gotten it yet. The best way to really master any concept is to teach it to someone else, because you have to then break that content into bite-sized bits and lead the person you're teaching through all the steps. You also have to figure out different ways to present the content, because what works for one student may not work for another.

This will really challenge those advanced students. And studies have shown that this kind of instruction is beneficial for both tutor and tutee.

"The students who had engaged in peer learning scored significantly higher on the QRI (Quality Reading Inventory) test than the students who had not, indicating the effectiveness peer tutoring can have on academic achievement." – Saga Briggs[13]

CHAPTER 7: PROBLEM SOLVING AND EDUCATION

"If we can shape the beliefs of children early enough to see problems as opportunities rather than dangers to be avoided, we can prepare them to meet a future in which the world is constantly shifting and what works today may not work tomorrow."
- Anton Anthony, Ed. S
Loving Education

So what is our educational system focusing on currently? We're focused on getting kids ready for college so they can earn degrees that may or may not prepare them for the future but are nearly guaranteed to put them in debt.

Twenty years ago, you didn't need a degree in social media marketing because social media didn't exist. A report released by Dell Computers in 2017 stated that 85 percent of jobs that will exist in the future haven't even been invented yet.

There are many who argue that people of the future won't have jobs at all. They will be replaced by robots and computer programs.

Educating for the Future

There is one thing that will always be true no matter how technologically advanced civilization becomes: humanity will always have problems and will always need people who can solve them.

That is what entrepreneurs do. They locate problems and they find solutions. They then trade those solutions for money. Training kids to be entrepreneurs, then, is the best way to prepare them to meet the future, no matter what that future might hold.

It is also the best way to help them improve their mindset about the problems they face in their life. If we can teach them from a very early age that every problem is just an opportunity in disguise, they will not be stopped by problems. They will be excited and challenged by them. Solve the problem for yourself or for someone else, and you can sell that solution and make money or trade that solution for something you need in return.

The brain is a massive supercomputer that is dedicated to helping the individual survive. The purpose of the imagination is to project possible outcomes so you can anticipate and prepare for problems as well as capitalize on opportunities that might come your way. Memory helps you avoid things that hurt you in the past and seek out more of what benefited you. Creativity helps you to innovate and create new things or find new ways around problems you encounter.

As with all computers, the brain has its own operating system. That operating system is made up of the things that you believe to be true based on your brain's analysis of the meaning behind the events that have happened to you in the past. This belief-based operating system begins development at conception and continues developing roughly through age twenty-two.

It is tested from age twenty-two until about age twenty-eight. During the testing phase, the things you believe are taken out and tested to see whether they still hold true or not. After that, it operates largely in the background, unnoticed and unchallenged, making decisions for you without your even being aware of it.

If we can shape the beliefs of children early enough to see problems as opportunities rather than dangers to be avoided, we can prepare them to meet a future in which the world is constantly shifting and what works today may not work tomorrow. Those early beliefs will give them a more positive outlook on life, too.

Removing the Fear of Failure

Failure is part of learning. Every baby fails thousands of times, at least, before they succeed in walking. Our current educational system, though, punishes failure. It creates this fear of failure where failure is seen as a sign that there is something wrong with the kid or that the kid did something wrong.

This fear of failure prevents kids from having the courage to take risks and try different things. It prevents them from being innovative and creative. If we want kids prepared for the future, we have to change the way we handle failure.

Failure is not bad. It is a learning opportunity. It just tells you that you haven't mastered the topic yet. There's nothing wrong with that. It tells you what you don't know.

Right now, we terrorize kids with these tests. "If you don't do well on this test, you're going to fail. You're going to be held back."

Students can fail every single class but pass the test and, in most cases, be promoted to the next grade.This is especially true here in Georgia. There's no effort to examine the kid's progress or to reward them for their effort in learning. That needs to change.

The "No Child Behind" laws were implemented to try to make sure that every child had access to a good, solid education. Unfortunately, it only served to leave more children behind than ever before while making teachers and schools afraid to try anything new for fear it would make things worse.

I play a part in evaluating teachers, and according to the Georgia Department of Education, teachers in Georgia are evaluated by the Teacher Keys Effectiveness System. There are three components teachers will be scored on: Teacher Assessment on Performance Standards,Professional Growth, and Student Growth.

Very soon, a part of every teacher's evaluation will be based on a test given at the end of the year. Although students will be scored and compared to the growth model of their peers, what are we really accomplishing? Will students be reading on grade level, or does it even matter anymore?

Are we, as an educational system, still continuing to focus on a test? Or are we focusing on truly moving and benefiting each student? The work is difficult, but moving students forward and educating them should be our main focus as educators.

Testing has its place, but it's a snapshot of a single moment in time. If you want a more accurate picture, you need a pre-test at the beginning of the year and a post-test at the end of the year.

For students, look for the progress that child has made throughout the year. Is the child's progress moving in a positive direction? How does it compare to the previous year's progress? A lot of times, things at home have a huge impact on a student's scores.

For example, if Mom and Dad got divorced in the middle of the year, you can expect that a student might even regress some from where they were at the beginning of the year. That negative progress signals a problem in the child's life that needs to be addressed. It may have absolutely nothing to do with the ability of the teacher or the quality of the educational program.

To evaluate teachers, look at the overall progress that the students have made in that teacher's class throughout the year. Are the majority of students making positive progress in their studies? That teacher is obviously doing something right and should be commended.

Sometimes a teacher will get a group of students who are two or three grade levels behind when they hit her class, and she still manages to bring them up to grade level by the end of the year. Instead of being recognized for her achievement, she is chastised or her pay is reduced because she didn't have them ready for the next year. This does nothing to encourage educators.

Schools, too, should be judged based on the progress made by buildings as a whole. How far did teachers get? How far did the students get?

The consequences for failure shouldn't be reductions in pay or even holding students back. When schools or teachers or students fail to make the expected progress, it is an opportunity to have a conversation about what went wrong and then work together to fix the problems. It's time for interventions and support systems to be put into place, not for punishments.

Encouraging Collaboration

Teaching kids how to work with other people, especially people with whom they do not agree or who have different beliefs than they do, is an essential part of any education. People who don't learn how to work with people who don't agree with them won't be able to hold down a job for long or keep a business going.

Relationships are the key to success in every area of life. There are seven billion people on this planet. It is virtually guaranteed that whatever you need in life, one of those people out there has it. Relationships are the key to convincing them to cooperate with you in achieving any goal.

For kids to be successful in collaborating, they need to be taught basic relationship skills. They often aren't seeing normal, healthy, functional relationships at home, so they aren't getting the opportunity to observe and model what those look like. Collaboration gives them a chance to practice the relationship skills being taught in the classroom in a practical manner.

And this is not just a problem for poor kids, inner city kids, or special needs kids. This is a problem that affects the smartest and brightest students just as much as the slowest kids in the class, and sometimes more.

I see it every day in the education field. You have these smart individuals with doctorate degrees in this or that. They are very intelligent. They can write papers and they can write theses. They can put together great dissertations, but at the end of the day they don't understand people and they don't know how to work with them.

They don't understand how to get along with the people who aren't like them. They have these amazing ideas that never become reality because they can't get the cooperation of other people to help support them in the areas where they are weak.

Children need to be taught to value each person in the class and to respect everyone. They never know who might have the answers or the resources they need. They must be given opportunities to work with people they don't agree with and not always be allowed to choose their teammates.

Seeing the Opportunity In Problems

As I mentioned earlier, kids need to be taught to see the opportunities present in the problems that face them. They need to be taught to look for the positive that goes with every negative.

Math, specifically Algebra, teaches us this vital lesson. Zero is level ground. You can build up from that point and make things positive, or you can dig down and make things negative.

Every shovelful of dirt removed from the ground is a negative. But for every shovelful of negative, there is a matching amount of positive. You add the two together and you are back on level ground. What you do from that point is up to you.

The hardest kids to teach are the ones that are going through so much negative in their lives that they are having trouble finding that positive. We need to be that positive force in their lives that helps to counteract all that negative.

We need to show them how to find the good in the middle of all the bad. We need to show them how to take the things that have happened to them and use them as a force that moves them forward rather than holds them back.

One of the ways we can do that is to help them use their talents—whether it's writing or singing or rapping or dancing or playing an instrument—to transform the pain they feel inside into something that helps other people get through their own pain. That way, they can take that negative experience and make it positive for someone else and for themselves at the same time.

Guiding Students In Problem Solving

Writing a book is all about solving a problem. You start with the problem and how that problem is making the person who is experiencing it feel: mad, sad, frustrated, disappointed, discouraged, or whatever the case may be. For example, the teacher in the classroom who is frustrated and discouraged because they can't get the kids in their class motivated to learn.

Then you move on to what that person wants to feel and what they think the solution is going to be. The truth about problems, though, is that we don't actually know what it is going to take to solve our problem, otherwise we'd have already solved it.

We just THINK we know. That's because we usually are focusing on the wrong problem. What we think is the problem isn't usually the actual problem. It's usually just a symptom of the actual problem. As an example, the fever isn't the actual problem when you're sick, it's just a symptom of the actual problem. However, most of us focus on fixing the fever instead of fixing the actual problem.

You, the writer, need to know what the real problem is and what the real solution is. You need to know what the obstacle is that is standing between your hero and the real solution.

Most teachers with unmotivated kids in the classroom, for instance, think that the problem would be solved if the PARENTS would just get involved or if they just had more money for better books and better supplies. What they don't know, though, is that that isn't their real problem.

Next, you identify how the reader wants to feel. In this case, these teachers want to feel appreciated, valued, and like they are making a difference.

Now you address what they are currently doing and the results they are getting. What is missing from those results? What is it that's leaving them unsatisfied about those results?

What teachers are currently doing to try to motivate students is usually: 1) Punishing students for misbehavior; 2) Fussing at kids for not participating; and 3) Talking to parents to try to get them to fix the problem.

The results of that are: 1) Kids resent you; 2) Kids are even less motivated to perform for you; 3) Parents are tired of hearing from you.

I propose that the real reason kids are not motivated is that: 1) They don't understand why they need what you are teaching; 2) They don't believe that you care about them; and 3) They don't like the way you are presenting the material.

After this, you lay out your solution and the results you know that solution is going to provide. I am suggesting that if you demonstrate the value of the material you are teaching in a way that is meaningful and fun to them, and you show them that you truly do have their best interests in heart, you will find that kids become excited to be in your class. You don't have to work so hard to motivate the students, and students perform better.

You also bring up the objections you are most likely to encounter to adopting that solution and answer those objections. I know that most teachers are going to think this doesn't apply to THEIR kids. They may also doubt that it will work at their school. Finally, they may simply not know how to do what I am suggesting they do.

My answers, as you have read, are that kids are kids no matter where they go to school. I have proven this will work in any school. And, lastly, I have presented all the ways that teachers can do what I've suggested they do.

Finally, you present the picture of what life is going to be like for your reader once your solution is in place and they are getting the results you've promised. Once you have adopted my solution, your kids are going to be excited and eager to learn from you, you're going to feel better about your teaching, parents are going to be more appreciative of the work you do, and your test results will improve, all at the same time.

These are the steps you take when you know what the problem's solution is. If you don't know, you take the writer's path:

1) Identify what you believe the problem is.
2) Think about how that problem makes you

feel.

3)   List out what you've done to try and solve the problem.

4)   Present the results of those attempts.

5)   Ask yourself what was missing from those results. Why weren't you happy with those results?

6)   What was it you wanted to happen?

7)   Find other people who have solved the problem you want to solve—or one like it— and ask them what they did to solve the problem.

8)   Test the answers you get until you find the best one for you.

CHAPTER 8. STOPPPING PROBLEMS BEFORE THEY BEGIN

"If this problem is happening over and over again, track down the source of the problem and do your best to address it."
- Anton Anthony, Ed. S
Loving Education

A lot of principals and educators wait until problems happen before they take action to stop them. I am the opposite. I am always looking for ways that I can stop problems before they begin. When you do that, it's easier to create the kind of environment where kids look forward to coming to school.

If the school or classroom is having the same common complaints, then we need to be putting together strategies to overcome those complaints rather than just letting them continue to build and build and build. If you have the same discipline issues grade after grade after grade, the problem isn't the students. There's a break down in the system somewhere.

Troubleshooting Problems

I do a lot of troubleshooting. It's about being proactive, rather than reactive. If we have a problem, I say, "Let's troubleshoot. Let's figure out what's happening so it won't happen again."

A lot of problems come because we're not troubleshooting and fixing the root of the problem. Instead, we're troubleshooting and then putting a band-aid on it. We don't actually fix the problem. We're just reacting and adding more fuel to the fire.

We could stop so many of the problems that happen in the classroom if we could just analyze why the problem is happening in the first place. A lot of the ineffective teachers and administrators are not troubleshooting. They're just trying to force things to work.

It's kind of like back in the old day when you had a messed-up TV. If it messed up, you started banging on the side of the set, hoping it would fix it. Sometimes it worked. Sometimes you made it worse.

The reason it was messing up was because there was a short in the circuitry. The reason that banging on the side of it seemed to fix the problem was because sometimes it would cause the wire that was out of place to connect again. However, that banging didn't fix the short circuit, and eventually the set would go out and stop working entirely.

That's what's going on in a lot of classrooms. Parents, administrators, and teachers are not dealing with the issues. They are just letting things go. They act like there's nothing I can do about it.

There's always something that can be done to make things better and to try to fix the problems. You can't fix everything, but you can try to put some things in place to help.

If you are an administrator and you have an ineffective teacher, it's not enough to just tell them to get better. Put some interventions in place to help make that teacher better. Send them to professional development or put the teacher through personal learning to help them address their weak points.

Try to figure out what's going on and why. It's easier to do that with students. You can find out just from talking to them what's going on in their lives. They'll tell you, to the best of their ability, what happened.

Sometimes the problem with a kid is the teacher. The teacher may yell or fuss and it triggers them. Students are then set off on a path of destruction just from a teacher fussing. I fixed a lot of problems like this just by moving a kid. A kid who use to misbehave in one teacher's class never had another issue once they were in another teacher's class. That's how I knew the problem was the teacher.\

The point is that you can't turn a blind eye and not address the situation or fix it. You have to look the problem in the eye and say, "Hey, this is the problem. Let's see how can I help you to fix it."

That's what I do now because I can't just go and rip teachers apart and put "You're a horrible teacher" on their evaluations. I have to offer support and interventions to help teachers get better instead of putting a band-aid on the problem by closing the teacher up in the room and saying, "Oh, well. I'm glad I'm not those students in her classroom. My God!" Instead, I troubleshoot to figure out what's wrong and then I take action to do something about it.

Educate People

One of the many lessons I learned from my years of experience in business is that a lot of problems can be solved with a little bit of education. Many problems are created because people don't understand the process, don't know how to give you what you need to do the work they want you to do, or don't understand why you are asking them to do what you want them to do. Kids aren't any different.

They need to know what the point is of the things you are asking them to do, they need to know what you need from them and how to give you what you want, and they need to understand how what you are asking them to do is going to benefit them.

A perfect example of this comes from a friend of mine who used to work at a custom greeting card company. Marketing departments would order custom cards from this company and pay about $4,000 for 1,000 cards. They would send those cards out to all their clients. These were really fancy cards and they would often want the signatures of the company owners or employees scanned in and printed on the cards.

One of the problems that kept coming up was the secretaries would use gel pens. The problem with gel pens is that they are not good scanning material, so signatures would come through broken up or unclear and unusable. Then the designer would have to either do a lot of work to fix the signatures or delay printing while they worked with the secretary to try and get more usable signatures.

Another problem that kept coming up was that the secretaries didn't understand the difference between Internet resolution and print resolution. If you want to print something, it needs to be a minimum of 300 dots per inch (DPI). Screens don't have that issue. Those screens can afford to have a smaller number of pixels. If you try to print something that was scanned in at less than 300 DPI, it will come out grainy and pixelated.

Nobody was taking the time to explain this to the secretaries, so we were having this problem over and over again. It could have been solved with a simple blog post or a short video educating them in what to do and how to do it.

That's the kind of thing teachers and educators need to think about doing. If this problem is happening over and over again, track down the source of the problem and do your best to address it.

Many times, it's simply a matter of education. Educate parents, educate students, educate teachers, educate whoever it is that's directly involved in the problem. Don't assume that they know what you know, because that's usually not true.

As I said earlier, if kids are constantly misbehaving, I step into the classroom and explain the rules to them. I don't hold them to the expectation of following a rule they don't know exists. I give them the chance to fix their behavior first.

Once I'm finished explaining the rules, though, I hold them accountable for following it. And I'm consistent in my expectations. They are always expected to follow it. I don't let things slide.

Look at the problems that are happening consistently if you're having the same problem appear over and over again. Figure out where the problem is coming from and how you can stop it before it even gets started.

Being Proactive

The first thing a principal should look at is the data. Know all of the students that are struggling and are already two or three grade levels behind. If it's a building-wide thing, address the problem building wide by implementing interventions to help the students as a whole.

For example, if we have about seventy to eighty percent of all students in the building who are reading two or three grade levels behind, or doing math two or three grade levels behind, make sure that there are interventions put into place for those students. Do what you can to support each and every child.

If you're a teacher, make an impact the best way you can. You can't control your boss or your boss's boss. You can only control what you can control and support the kids you can support and take away what you can take away from this.

Learn what you can so that when you make it to the next step, whether you are principal or whatever that next step in your career maybe, you can show that you did what you could do to help better serve your students, the parents, and the other teachers around you.

Any school can be turned into a magnet school within three years if the right support and interventions are put into place. This is my biggest pet peeve with all administrators. We have to make the school function like the kids don't have any support at home and give them everything we possibly can give them, and more, inside the four walls of our school.

As soon as the bell rings, the interventions need to begin and we need to be teaching instruction. That's why I gave my kids time for downtime, socialization, and parties last year. We found a reason to celebrate every day because I wanted every day, Monday through Friday, to provide the kids what they needed

By the time the kids hit the door, let's give them what they need. Let's drill. Let's remediate. Let's motivate. Let's give them the curriculum that they need. I don't want people to say that it's the school's fault and that we're failing them. I can't control every building, but principals have a lot of power to make the changes that need to be made.

You have to be proactive. I taught school-wide behavior from day one because you can't wait to start teaching behavior in week six. You can't be reactive to kids because they need to learn. I didn't want to wait until they got into fights and their behavior was uncontrollable before I took action.

Take a Top-Down Approach

Unfortunately, superintendents sometimes put the wrong people in the wrong places. The principals are the ones who are really in charge of a building. They have the power to affect the lives of the students and the teachers. If I were superintendent, I would be very selective about the people that I put in charge of these schools.

Principals, in turn, have to make sure that they're hiring the right teachers who are the right fit for their building, teachers who will help them change the culture of the school and help to build up the students. Even though making changes starts with the classroom, the teachers know that it really starts at the top and then trickles down into the classrooms.

Teachers are only given the visions of the principals and have to work to implement that vision. Principals are only given the visions of the superintendents. The superintendents are only given the visions of the community and the school board members. It trickles down to the county from the state, and the state is going to do what it's going to do.

Putting the right people in the right places is very important. It's the key to the success of the educational system and the success of our nation. A lot of teachers are frustrated when they watch principals put in classrooms teachers who shouldn't even be teachers. They are hired based on their credentials and degrees but can't relate to the students they are teaching.

Teachers should be carefully selected for the area they are teaching. You can't take a high school teacher and make them an elementary or pre-K teacher. It takes a special gift to relate to pre-K kids. You have to know how to console and talk to those kids and teach them things.

It's very hard to take a middle school teacher and make them an elementary or high school teacher. There are some teachers that can go from middle to high school without a problem. That's not usual, though.

Teaching is a profession where you really have to want to do it. You have to have a love of kids. That's where the educational system is going wrong, because a lot of teachers are just getting into the profession for the schedule, not for the students. They are being hired for their degrees and credentials, not for the passion they have for the kids and the teaching.

A lot of the older teachers are retiring and getting out. Those older teachers were the ones that had that passion. They were the one that would do it without a check.

They were paid next to nothing. They made it happen with the bare minimum. Those were the teachers that cared about the kids.

Now you are getting teachers that come in because of summer vacations. That's becoming a prevalent thing when people are looking at what they want to do in life. They think they want to be teachers, but that's not how education should be.

Don't Pass Along Problems

Another big problem is that we're just pushing students along and we're creating a bigger failure by pushing students along who can't read, can barely write, and struggle to do basic math. We put a test in front of them and we push them along whether they pass or fail because we don't want to be held accountable for failing all these kids.

This is what the educational system has turned into. In certain districts in Georgia, you can only give a kid a fifty-five. It doesn't matter if a kid comes into your class and doesn't do anything. You can't give them less than a fifty-five.

If a kid sits in your class and goes to sleep or tells you that he's not going to do the work, you cannot put a zero in the book. You can't give them less than a fifty-five.

The logic behind that is that if a child decides in that first nine weeks to buckle down and do some work, if you give that child a zero, it is almost impossible for him to pass that class with a seventy. I understand why the rule is in place.

However, it's unfair to the kid that's actually trying his hardest and earns a fifty-five. When that kid is giving you his best, but his best is a fifty-five, and then you have somebody in the back of your classroom who refuses to do anything and you have to give him the same grade, it's just not right. We need to re-evaluate how we're handling those students so that we aren't the problem.

Creating A Sense of Safety

School must be a safe place. A lot of parents are not teaching the appropriate behavior, so we can't assume we're going to walk into a class and every student is willing and able to learn. Everybody is able to learn, but sometimes they're not willing to learn from you because they don't trust you.

We have to create that sense of safety for that child. That's the reason I got into administration: because I wanted to be that leader who could build not just a classroom or a hallway, but an entire building of safety for the students. When I was principal, I had kids that hated to miss school just because it was the only safe place in their world.

I want everyday, all 180 days, to be positive experiences. I want the kids to say, "You know what? I remember my principal, Mr. Anthony."

I want to be remembered like certain people remember teachers who made a difference in their lives, like Mr. Sams, Mr. Ishmal, and Mrs. Cummings made in my life. I don't remember any of my principals like that. I remember teachers because I saw them everyday, but I want students to be able to see me provide a positive experience.

I want them to say, "You know, I loved middle school. I want to go back to middle school because of Mr. Anthony. I'm inspired in life because I want to be a leader in the community."

They don't have to be like me,;they could be great in their own field, and be a leader who inspires other kids like I inspire them. I'm passionate about this. I love it!

I've worked a lot of jobs, but if you take away the kids, I would quit. They are the ones who make my job really worth doing. The adults are the ones that tend to get on my nerves. It's not the kids.

Even when the kids have a little drama, I like doing experiments to see why kids behave certain ways. Almost every single time it's not what happens at the school that leads to the trouble. It's often something either at home or that happened in the neighborhood and it just boils over at the school. We just catch the tail end of it.

Think about this. The major trouble that kids get into, whether it's fights, or guns, or weapons, or drugs, where did they get that stuff?

The guns and the weapons they usually get from home. We don't create guns and weapons at school. We don't create drugs at school. They bring it from home or from the neighborhood. Kids are only doing what they do outside of school. That's where they learn this stuff.

Parents also tend to teach their kids how to handle bullying and violence the wrong way. They tell them that if they get hit, to hit back, so I have to go in classrooms all the time to teach them the right way to handle things. I tell kids that we have to learn to respond to things that may make us upset in the adult way. They are kids, but I tell them, "If you walk up to Mr. Anthony and you slap me, I'm not gonna hit you back. I'm gonna call the police and I'm going to press charges. You're going to get fired from your job. You might go to jail.

Now, if someone slaps you in school, we are your police. We work for you. You need to call administration and let us handle it. I will investigate and I will suspend the person who is guilty. I will do these things because that's my job."

If a school is horrible and if students are fighting all the time, if there is no cohesion, and kids know there is going to be a ruckus everyday in school or in class, they're not going to learn, because they want to see who's going to fight. They want to go disrupt the class. There's no learning taking place, because they are always running amuck.

That's why I set building-wide expectations for how the kids would behave from the bus line to the classroom. It changed the climate of that school because kids knew there were certain things I would not allow.

In my year of being a principal, I led that building-wide climate and culture shift, focused on changing the student's mindsets, and my building was running to the point where I didn't have to worry about fights, fussing, cussing, or disruptions. The academic achievement in the classroom improved right along with it because you could get more done.

Making Small Changes For Big Impacts

As a principal of a middle school, one of the small changes that I made to the building schedule that made a major impact was in the way students moved between classes. A lot of the trouble that students get into is when they are moving from one class to another.

Decreasing the amount of unsupervised transitions decreased the amount of behavioral incidents tremendously. The more kids move, the more chances they have to get into trouble.

I took that time that I freed up and applied it to building-wide remediation for those students who were struggling and acceleration classes if the kids were on track. Everyday for thirty minutes, everybody was either going to be doing some type of reading or math remediation or acceleration. That thirty minutes of the day was sacred, with no building-wide movement.

I created a climate and a culture where kids knew we don't fight here. I told them, "If you fight in my building and you're causing a disruption, that's a public disruption (a public disruption was a major infraction). I wanted students to think as adults and I provided them with real-world examples. I told students this: If your parents go to Walmart and fought the manager, what would happen to your parents? They would be arrested. We have to treat school like the real world. Teach them, share with them, and show them.

As a principal, I went in learning the kids, learning about their behavior problems, looking at the building-wide data in the summertime before a single child ever stepped into my building. I knew what I was going to do to teach them before school began.

Giving Feedback

Students across America and across the world look at their teachers, and all they want is for their teacher to be happy with them. They will try to do their best once they know you care, because they crave that feedback. They want to see "Good job." They even want to know if there are areas where they can improve.

Students want that feedback from us. Good or bad, they want to see how they can make us happy as individuals. If teachers across the nation and the world knew how much of an impact that praise and that guidance makes in the life of their students, I think we would give them more of that feedback that they so long to receive. They often are not getting a lot of feedback when they go home.

Setting Consistent, Simple Rules

Another thing that needs to happen is that schools need to set consistent, simply understood rules, and there needs to be an assembly at the beginning of the year where those rules are set and laid out. As a principal in

Sumter County, Georgia, I did that and it cut down a lot of discipline problems before they had a chance to begin.

I don't like to be reactive, whether I'm running a school or running a classroom. I don't want to wait until something goes awry and then end up saying, "Oh, my God! Let's clean this up. Now let's react." I want to put systems into place that stop the problems before they can begin.

Put Me In the Game, Coach

Along my journey in education, I have played many different roles: teacher, coach, administrator, discipline coordinator, principal, and even parent. Of all those roles, I find quite often that the job of an administrator is more like being a coach.

Some people might be wondering, "What do you mean it's like being a coach?"

The job of a coach is to analyze the game, create a game plan, and then sometimes change that game plan based on how the players are doing. We scout other teams and we watch playback films to try and figure out a plan of action. Sometimes, as administrators, our

171

job is similar and goes hand and   hand with coaching.

During the summer we scout, we look at the data to see what support the students are going to need from us to do their best, and we put together a game plan based on that. That way, we are ready for the kids to enter our building.

Once the kids are in our building, though, sometimes we have to revisit that plan of action just like a coach may have to revise the game plan based on the performance of his team. As principal, there were many times I've realized I needed to change my game plan.

Sometimes, just as a coach may need to change the game plan several times during one game in order to win, I would have to change my game plan multiple times during the course of a day. No two days are ever alike in education, especially when you're dealing with kids.

You have to let your staff know to be ready to change the game plan, too. Teachers may plan a lesson one way, but at the end of the day, they may realize it didn't go as planned. Teachers need to be ready to regroup, rethink, and represent the material in order to help students succeed.

As principal, I can remember looking at my game plan in December and realizing that things hadn't gone as planned. Being the instructional leader, I realized that our schedule, or some things we'd planned to provide that remediation time for our students, needed to be revisited.

I scrapped the plan and we tabled it. We came back from the holidays. I showed it to the staff and asked for the feedback that I needed to revisit the plan so that our students got the support they needed. Everything you do as an administrator and everything you do in the classroom should be focused on benefitting the students. If it is not, your game plan needs to be changed.

Looking at that game plan, revisiting it to make sure that we focus on the rigor and the instruction that we need, should be the focus of education today. This is one of the things that we can do to change education and make it better for tomorrow.

CHAPTER 9. AA STEM ACADEMY

"I want them to see their creativity as a way to do something that will help other people be successful and get out of poverty."
- Anton Anthony, Ed. S
Loving Education

Through the experiences that I've had as a teacher, coach, discipline coordinator, assistant principal, and principal, I have encountered all different types of students, all different types of talent, and all different ability levels.

There are so many things that I feel that we're missing. My school would be for the students that are artistically gifted.

Most of these students, because they don't see anything in the neighborhood for them, are often the ones who ended up dropping out of school, joining gangs, or dealing drugs. Quite often, they don't see their gifts as a possible way out of poverty because the only paths to success that they see on TV are to become a football or basketball player or else to become a famous musician or a singer.

They don't realize that their talents and gifts can be used to help them start successful businesses of their own. The goal of my academy would be to show them how to take their gifts and talents and apply them to solving problems for other people in their community. That's what an entrepreneur is: someone who gets paid to solve problems for other people.

Identifying and Encouraging Talents

As principal, there was a little girl that inspired me so much. She tried out for Disney. She was so talented. She was in Americus, Georgia, in Sumter County. She was one of the young ladies that performed in one of the school songs. She was so talented. She was proud of that. She was probably the most talented kid that I've ever seen before in my life. But, you know, Disney gets so many people trying out. They don't really get to see the full talent because some people get nervous. When a person is truly comfortable with you, though, then they can really shine.

These kids are great basketball players and a lot of them are good football players, but the chances of them becoming professional athletes are slim to none. However, there are other talents that they have. A lot of them are great actors or singers or musicians and while they may never be able to make it all the way to Hollywood with those talents, they can put those skills to use in the service of their local community in other ways.

A lot of my students were talented to the point that they played several different instruments. Those who sang were in chorus, or they were in band, and had just amazing God -given gifts. Some of them couldn't sing or perform or play an instrument, but they could write. It is just incredible how many authors you have in a school, how many singers you have in a school, how many playwrights you have in a school, but they're not exposed to enough career paths to know how to take those things and make a living with them.

In the last couple of years, the music industry has changed. I'll say it like this: back in the day you had to find a music company to do the production for you. They would sign a deal and they would pay for you to go into a recording booth and do different things.

Now, you can record a song on your phone or on your iPad or on your laptop and it can blow up in a matter of minutes. You can use it to create YouTube videos, and a lot of people are blowing up on those things.

So my school would focus on those arts. It will be a Science, Technology, Engineering, and Math (STEM) focused school, but the technology piece will be in teaching the kids production. They will learn all the behind-the-scenes production elements such as video recording and editing, along with music recording and audio editing with graphic design.

Creative Application of Science and Math

A lot of the activities that I would be doing would include science. I would include experiments and creative activities. If you have a microscope in the room, let's pull out hair follicles and see what our hair is made of or let's see what our skin is made of. We would just see what different things around the room and around the world were made of.

We would focus on giving them real life and real world experiences in science and math. A lot of kids want to know, "What do I need to know this stuff for?"

I had one kid this week who got into some trouble and was mad. He said, "I don't want to be at school". He was one of my 504 students, which means he has some type of diagnosis like ADD, ADHD or maybe a physical impairment.

He was upset about class and about school. He told me, "I don't need school anymore. What do we need with school? I already know how to write. I know how to count."

He was serious. I told him, "Son, you are only in the sixth grade. There is so much that you have to learn. I understand that you don't like the procedures at school and that sometimes it can be a routine. I hate schools like that and I hate routines, too."

I hate it with a passion when you come in and you do the same thing. You open up to page twenty-five or whatever and just read in a book. I want learning to come alive for my students, even if it's just a book that you're reading. Let's make it come alive.

My school, like I said, will deal not only with music but also video production and movies. I want my students to be able to create a movie themselves and we will shop it. We will shop the movie, we will shop TV shows, impromptu shows, and our own productions.

It will be just like a regular studio, like Universal Studios, and we will pitch movies to those studios all day. I want to be able to pitch a movie to someone for my kids from my school and it actually goes somewhere. I know it can be done. These students are so creative. If you can think it, they can make it happen.

Applied Creativity

In the alternative school, one thing that the kids were familiar with was music. They were so big on music. They wanted to create beats and a lot of them wanted to be rappers. They would go in the street and rap about the street, the drugs, or whatever.

I heard some of the music created by the alternative school students. There was talent there. But sometimes when they left school, they would get lost in the world of the streets because they weren't offered the things they need. A lot of people that I talked to had to go outside and get in their studio time.

With the right resources, that desire could be used to channel their energy toward school so that all they want to do is come to school so that they could record and make music. They would be expected to go to class and do their work before they could go back into the studio. That would channel their focus on coming to school instead of being in the streets.

Their studies would not just focus on music and music production. The school would teach the students the full aspect of the music industry. They would learn the history of it and really study it and get into it.

And it would be that way with all the creative arts, from music and acting to writing and singing. The kids would be rewarded for doing well in their main studies by getting access to the recording studios and production areas. Their studies would focus in-depth on learning the history and the facts behind the industry.

Teaching Entrepreneurship

I want students to be focused on building that entrepreneurial mindset. It's not that all of them will go ahead and create a business, but developing that mindset and that go-getter attitude.

I want them to see their creativity as a way to do something that will help other people be successful and get out of poverty. I want them to see it as a path to a better future for themselves and their family.

That mindset is how you change a neighborhood or an environment. I wanted my school to be focused on creating that mindset, serving the community, and improving yourself. The reason why people get an education is to be valuable to the community and to their families, to become responsible citizens who have something of value to contribute, and who are ready and able to serve the needs of the community.

The more that kids know, the better they will do. The more knowledge kids have, the better they will turn out in life.

Community Collaboration

One of the ways my school will teach collaboration is to put together teams of students with different gifts to support one another. For example, the musician may support the writer by creating a themed album for the content the writer has written. The artist may design a cover for the writer and for the musician. If they all work together, everyone comes out ahead.

Another way that my school will teach collaboration is to provide small businesses with services they need like video editing, graphic design, jingle-writing and production, voice-over talents, and things of that nature. The school will charge a modest fee for the services the students provide, and in return the students don't have to pay to attend the school.

Impacting the Future

The students we produce today are the future. Giving these students, the hard students, the ones that nobody really wants, an education will be challenging, but if we can turn them around and change their lives, we will improve the community and impact the future in a very positive way. That's the goal of AA STEM Academy.

NOTES

1   Abraham H. Maslow, "A Theory of Human Motivation," Classics in the History of Psychology ~ A. H. Maslow (1943) A Theory of Human Motivation, August 2000, , accessed October 18, 2018, https://psychclassics. yorku.ca/Maslow/motivation.htm.

2   Harry Harlow, "The Nature of Love," Classics in the History of Psychology ~ Harlow (1958), March 2000, , accessed October 18, 2018, https://psychclassics.yorku. ca/Harlow/love.htm.

3   Harry Harlow, "The Nature of Love," Classics in the History of Psychology ~ Harlow (1958), March 2000, , accessed October 18, 2018, https://psychclassics.yorku. ca/Harlow/love.htm.

4   Harry Harlow, "The Nature of Love," Classics in the History of Psychology ~ Harlow (1958), March 2000, , accessed October 18, 2018, https://psychclassics.yorku. ca/Harlow/love.htm.

5   Katie Malinski, "The Kids Who Need the Most Love Will Ask for It in the Most Unloving Ways," Katie Malinski, LCSW, May 09, 2014, , accessed October 18, 2018, https://katiemalinski.com/2013/12/the-kids-who-need-the-most-love-will-ask-for-it-in-the-most-unloving-ways/).

6   Ayrum Weiss, "Love Is a Behavior," Psychology Today, August 2018, , accessed October 18, 2018, https://www.psychologytoday.com/us/blog/fear-intimacy/201808/love-is-behavior.

7   Norine R. Barnes, Why Do Children Misbehave? PDF, Denton, TX: Texas Agricultural Extension Service, September 2011.

8   Jane Meredith Adams, "Positive School Climate Boosts Test Scores, Study Says," EdSource, April 29, 2013, , accessed October 18, 2018, https://edsource.org/2013/positive-school-climate-boosts-test-scores-study-says/31043.

9   Saul McLeod, "Saul McLeod," Memory, Encoding Storage and Retrieval | Simply Psychology, January 01, 1970, , accessed October 18, 2018, https://www.simplyp-

sychology.org/memory.html.

10   Erin J. Wamsley and Robert Stickgold, "Dreaming and Offline Memory Processing," Current Biology : CB, December 07, 2010, , accessed October 19, 2018, https://www.ncbi.nlm.nih.gov/pmc/articles/PMC3557787/.

11   Annie Murphy Paul, "The Neuroscience of Your Brain on Fiction," The New York Times, March 17, 2012, , accessed October 19, 2018, https://www.nytimes.com/2012/03/18/opinion/sunday/the-neuroscience-of-your-brain-on-fiction.html.

12   Plato. Translated by Benjamin Jowett. "Introduction," The Republic. Provided by The Internet Classics Archive, Daniel C. Stevenson, Web Atomics. World Wide Web presentation. 360 B.CE. (http://classics.mit.edu//Plato/republic.html)

13   Saga Briggs, "How Peer Teaching Improves Student Learning and 10 Ways To Encourage It," InformED, March 24, 2017, , accessed October 19, 2018, https://www.opencolleges.edu.au/informed/features/peer-teaching/.

BIBLIOGRAPHY

Adams, Jane Meredith. "Positive School Climate Boosts Test Scores, Study Says." EdSource. April 29, 2013. Accessed October 18, 2018. https://edsource.org/2013/positive-school-climate-boosts-test-scores-study-says/31043.

Barnes, Norine R. Why Do Children Misbehave? PDF. Denton, TX: Texas Agricultural Extension Service, September 2011.
http://denton.agrilife.org/files/2011/09/behaviorproblemsinchildren_1.pdf

Briggs, Saga. "How Peer Teaching Improves Student Learning and 10 Ways To Encourage It." InformED. March 24, 2017. Accessed October 19, 2018. https://www.opencolleges.edu.au/informed/features/peer-teaching/.

Harlow, Harry. "The Nature of Love." Classics in the History of Psychology ~ Harlow (1958). March 2000. Accessed October 18, 2018. https://psychclassics.yorku.ca/Harlow/love.htm.
First published in American Psychologist, 13, 673-685

Malinski, Katie. "The Kids Who Need the Most Love Will Ask for It in the Most Unloving Ways." Katie Malinski, LCSW. May 09, 2014. Accessed October 18, 2018. https://katiemalinski.com/2013/12/the-kids-who-need-the-most-love-will-ask-for-it-in-the-most-unloving-ways/).

Maslow, Abraham H. "A Theory of Human Motivation." Classics in the History of Psychology ~ A. H. Maslow (1943) A Theory of Human Motivation. August 2000.

Accessed October 18, 2018. https://psychclassics.yorku.
ca/Maslow/motivation.htm.
Originally Published in Psychological Review, 50, 370-
396.

McLeod, Saul. "Saul McLeod." Memory, Encoding Stor-
age and Retrieval | Simply Psychology. January 01, 1970.
Accessed October 18, 2018. https://www.simplypsycholo-
gy.org/memory.html.

Paul, Annie Murphy. "The Neuroscience of Your Brain
on Fiction." The New York Times. March 17, 2012.
Accessed October 19, 2018. https://www.nytimes.
com/2012/03/18/opinion/sunday/the-neuroscience-of-
your-brain-on-fiction.html.

Plato. "The Republic." The Internet Classics Archive |
The Republic by Plato. 1994. Accessed October 18, 2018.
http://classics.mit.edu//Plato/republic.html

Wamsley, Erin J., and Robert Stickgold. "Dreaming and
Offline Memory Processing." Current Biology : CB.
December 07, 2010. Accessed October 19, 2018. https://
www.ncbi.nlm.nih.gov/pmc/articles/PMC3557787/.

Weiss, Ayrum. "Love Is a Behavior." Psychology Today.
August 2018. Accessed October 18, 2018. https://www.
psychologytoday.com/us/blog/fear-intimacy/201808/
love-is-behavior.

ABOUT THE AUTHOR

Anton Anthony, Ed. S has served in school districts throughout Georgia as a teacher, as a discipline coordinator, as a coach, as an assistant principal, and as a principal.

He has worked in poverty-stricken schools where the majority of the population was Title I. He has also worked in schools where parents were highly educated, high-income professionals and business owners. Each school brought its own challenges, but he was able to break through barriers and achieve academic improvement everywhere he went.

Credentials

Mr. Anthony received his Bachelor of Arts with Honors in Business Management from Fort Valley State University in Georgia. He received his Masters of Arts in Teaching at Augusta State University.

He later went back to receive a degree in Curriculum and Instruction from Augusta University and received his Educational Specialist add on in Educational Leadership and Administration, also at Augusta University. He is a licensed educator and real estate broker with the State of Georgia.

Career

He began his educational career in Burke County, Georgia schools as a reading specialist who was moved into the 7th grade English/Language arts program (ELA), where he experienced his first real taste of educational success. His class achieved the highest passing percentage, and he was given an award to recognize his achievement.

After spending a second year at the middle school where he began his career, he asked for a position as coach at an alternative school in that same district. Former teacher of the year for the school, he was afforded the opportunity to become not only the coach, but the discipline coordinator, and reading instructor.

From those positions, he would go on to become an assistant principal and principal. In order to be closer to his own children, he currently is an school administrator for Richmond County School System in Augusta, Georgia.

Current Status

Mr. Anthony currently lives in Augusta, Georgia. He is one of the most active administrators on social media and looks forward to bringing his vision of AA STEM Academy to life.

Contact Information

To connect with Mr. Anthony, you can find him online.
Facebook:

https://www.facebook.com/LovingEducation-Book

Twitter:
https://Twitter.com/antonanthony5

Instagram:
http://Instagram.com/authorantonanthony

LinkedIn:
http://www.linkedin.com/in/authorantonan-thonysr

YouTube:
https://www.youtube.com/channel/UCI77nqy8OXItxQ_ZazNSm0w

Email:
AAStemAcademy@gmail.com
antonanthonysr@gmail.com

FREE OFFER

Visit http://authorantonanthony.com/books to get a FREE INTEREST INVENTORY to help you start applying Loving Education to your school or classroom today! You can print as many copies of the interest inventory as you need.

Use it to get to know your students better, especially those hard-to-reach students. You can also become part of the Loving Education Movement by joining our FREE Facebook group, Loving Education Resources. Get the help, support, and advice you need to improve your school or classroom. For more useful tips about applying Loving Education to your school or classroom, follow the Loving Education Facebook page (https://www.facebook.com/LovingEducation-Book)

Buyers Appreciated, Reviewers Adored!

Leaving a review takes only a moment of your time but can make a huge difference in the number of people who see, and know about, this book. Please consider leaving a review on the site where you purchased the book or on our Facebook Fan Page "Loving Education". Every review counts!